Route of the Eagles

Missouri Pacific in the Streamlined Era

by Greg Stout

FOR MY DAD - WHO I HOPE IS PROUD

WHITERIVER
PRODUCTIONS
6545 Scenic Drive, Kansas City, MO 64133

Route of the Eagles
Missouri Pacific in the Streamlined Era

© White River Productions, 1995

Published by White River Productions, 6545 Scenic Drive, Kansas City, Missouri 64133.

Printed and bound in the United States of America.

ISBN: 0-89745-99-1

Editor: Kevin EuDaly

Editorial assistance was provided by John Mills, Alan W. Hegler, Charlie Duckworth, and Lon EuDaly.

Layout & Artwork by Kevin EuDaly

Cartography by Matt Kauffman

Contents

Acknowledgments

No work of history, even one as humble as this, is the work of a single individual. Instead, the researcher relies upon the generous assistance of countless historians, photographers, librarians, proofreaders and editors, each of whom helps to shape his efforts into a comprehensible whole. Such has been the case in this instance.

In working on *Route of the Eagles*, I have been twice blessed: First, by the many historians, photographers and collectors who have graciously submitted the slides, photographs and anecdotes that have brought this book to life. And second, by those unselfish individuals who have edited and corrected the multiple drafts this book went through before reaching final form.

To all the wonderful people who helped, including Charlie Duckworth, Joe Collias, Ray Curl, Larry Thomas, George Drake, Sr., John Mills, Dan Pope, Randy Drolen, Alan Wayne Hegler, J. Parker Lamb, Paul Meyer, Ed Keilty, Bert Pennypacker, John Eagan, Bill Herbert, and Ray George, I am deeply indebted. Thanks must also go to Jerry Howe, Missouri Pacific Historical Society Archivist, Richard Ryker, Union Pacific librarian, Paulette Biedenbender, Trains Magazine editorial assistant, and to my friend and publisher, Kevin EuDaly, for their work. Finally, thanks to Howard Eldridge for his assistance, and to my wife, Carol, for her patience and encouragement throughout this project.

Finally, a hearty thanks to the photographers who submitted material for possible inclusion in this effort, including:

Ken Albrecht	Joe McMillan
Ralph Back	Paul Meyer
Steve Beleck	Jerry Michels
Alan Bradley	Dan Munson
Barry Carlson	William J. Neill
Joe Collias	Steve Patterson
Lon Coone	Jerry Pitts
Ray Curl	Dan Pope
Charlie Duckworth	Robert Seale
John Eagan	J. W. Swanberg
James EuDaly	Larry Thomas
James Holder	Robin Thomas
David Johnston	Harold K. Vollrath
Peter Kane	Dick Wallin
David King	John Wegner
J. Parker Lamb	J. Harlen Wilson
Bob Malinoski	Charles Zeiler
Louis Marre	Gary Zuters

Above: Companion trains to the *Missouri River Eagles* on the Kansas City- St. Louis route were afternoon mail runs 15-14. In this photo No. 14 waits at Kansas City Union Station for her 4:00pm departure time. The hogger will need every one of those 5,000 EMD horses if he's going to keep the fourteen car consist on the advertised. *Art Riordan photo, John Eagan collection*

Front dust jacket and page 1: The streamlined era on the MoPac started with the *Eagle*, shown behind E3 7001. The new trainset is on one of its publicity runs on the Eastern Division at Bridge 14A just east of South Point, Missouri, three miles east of Washington. The bleak hillsides are under the grip of winter prior to the March 10, 1940 inauguration of the *Eagle*, as the train poses for the ACF photographer. *ACF photo, Joe Collias collection*

Foreword

Passenger service on the Missouri Pacific Lines traced its origins to the period immediately following the Civil War, when trains began operating between St. Louis and Kansas City, Missouri. In the years that followed, new trackage and new trains sprang up regularly, until the MoPac eventually fielded a vast network of public conveyances over main lines and branches between the Mississippi River, the Gulf of Mexico and the Continental Divide. Today, the tradition of service continues (though in much diminished form) via Amtrak services on the lines between St. Louis-Kansas City and St. Louis-Texas.

During their time as private carriers, the Missouri Pacific, Texas & Pacific, Gulf Coast Lines, C&EI and Iron Mountain served up many excellent trains; however, none were finer or more famous than the Raymond Loewy-designed *Eagle* fleet that first took to the rails in 1940. By means of a complex series of connections and through car operations, the *Eagles* reached from their principal home in St. Louis to cities as far

afield as New York, Baltimore, Chicago, Houston, Mexico City, New Orleans, Denver and Los Angeles. As a result, the photographs chosen for this work represent the efforts of lensmen as diverse and talented as Colorado's Otto Perry, Texas' J. Parker Lamb and St. Louis' Joe Collias, to name only a few. Sadly, however, because I did not reach for a camera until 1969, and then only to shoot Kodacolor, my own work is not represented in this volume.

Route of the Eagles is organized into chapters covering the Missouri Pacific's major passenger lines: West from St. Louis to Kansas City, Omaha and Colorado; south, from St. Louis and Memphis to Louisiana, Texas and Mexico; and across the length of the Lone Star State (and a little more), from New Orleans to El Paso. In addition, because it came into the MoPac fold in 1967, a review of the Chicago & Eastern Illinois and its famous *Dixie* fleet is included. We'll also pause along the way to check out competitors Wabash, Frisco, and Katy, and to stretch our legs at St. Louis and Kansas City Union Stations. To keep a manageable

scope, our history begins with the inaugural run of the first streamlined *Eagle* and ends, as it must, on Amtrak conveyance day in 1971.

Finally, although more than a year and a half of research went into putting this book together, errors in both fact and inference no doubt exist. To the degree that they do, they are solely my own responsibility, and I can only hope that they do not detract from the enjoyment of the overall work. So grab your suitcase, make sure you've got your ticket, and call a taxi for Union Station. You've got a space reserved aboard the *Eagle*, and you don't want to be late!

Below: A pair of PA's whisk No. 37 south at Texarkana, Arkansas on December 2, 1956. Nearly everything from this photograph is now gone. The gas station proudly displays gasoline available for 25 cents, the tire store has a good stock of wide whitewall tires, and there are no fewer than six Coke signs. *Joe Collias photo, Kevin EuDaly collection*

3

1   The Missouri Pacific Railroad

Like most major carriers, the Missouri Pacific that existed at the time of the Union Pacific merger was not built as a single property, but represented the amalgamation of several predecessor companies and short lines. Of the MoPac's antecedents, the most important were the Missouri Pacific itself, the St. Louis, Iron Mountain & Southern, the Texas & Pacific, the International-Great Northern, the Gulf Coast Lines and, after 1967, the Chicago & Eastern Illinois.

The Pacific Railroad of Missouri, the direct predecessor of the MoPac, was chartered by the Missouri General Assembly in March, 1849, to build a railroad from St. Louis to the western boundary of Missouri, and to connect there with any railroad built eastward from the Pacific Coast. The original charter was subsequently amended to allow the Pacific Railroad to build a line of its own all the way to the west coast.

The company was organized in St. Louis in January, 1850. Thomas Allen was named president and James Kirkwood was hired as chief engineer in charge of construction.

Mr. Kirkwood recommended a gauge of 5 feet 6 inches for the new railroad on the assumption that the first railroad west of the Mississippi was free to select the gauge "best suited to the mechanics of the problem." The 5-foot, 6-inch gauge was adopted by the Missouri legislature and made mandatory for all Missouri railroads. It was also adopted by the first Texas railroads. In July, 1869, the gauge of the Missouri Pacific was changed to 4'9", and still later to 4'8-1/2."

Ground was broken for the Pacific Railroad in St. Louis in July, 1851. Actual operations began a little more than a year later, in December, 1852. Construction west was slowed by the rugged terrain outside St. Louis, epidemics of cholera and labor shortages, and it was not until 1855 that the line reached the Missouri capitol at Jefferson City.

During the next ten years, construction proceeded westward, but due to continuous harassment by Confederate troops after 1860, track laying crews were unable to reach Kansas City until September 19, 1865. Daily service was inaugurated between the two cities on October 2, 1865.

In the same year the Pacific Railroad was chartered, the Missouri Legislature also granted a charter for construction of the St. Louis & Iron Mountain Railroad. The new road was to "sur-

vey, grade and construct" a line between St. Louis and Pilot Knob, Missouri, a distance of 85 miles.

The charter additionally gave the company the right to extend the line to Cape Girardeau, and to the southwestern border of the state within ten years. Construction rights were granted to the same leaders that had started the Pacific Railroad. James H. Morley, a protege of James Kirkwood, was named chief engineer of the Iron Mountain line. Like the Pacific Railroad, the original gauge of the Iron Mountain was 5'6". This was changed to standard 4'8-1/2" in June, 1879. During the interim, to facilitate car interchange with the Texas & Pacific and the International-Great Northern, a car hoist and transfer was constructed at Texarkana.

Below: No. 12 is doing a little left-hand running as it grinds its way up Kirkwood Hill on a mild morning in January, 1960, normal operation for the station stop since the depot is on the north side of the tracks. That dome-coach is one of the Pullman-Standard cars delivered in 1952 for the *Texas Eagles*. *J. Parker Lamb*

Above: It's October 5, 1968, and E8 41 is idling in a downpour on the point of a two-car No. 16 at Kansas City Union Station. The *Eagle* is scheduled for an 11:30am departure time, and barring the unexpected, she'll tie up in St. Louis, 279 miles to the east, at 5:10pm.
Joe McMillan

Following some contract improprieties on the part of the construction company, the Iron Mountain was forced to undertake completion of the work itself. As a result of the delay, the line was not opened to Pilot Knob until 1858. Fifteen years later, following consolidation with the Cairo and Fulton Railroad, the Iron Mountain reached Texarkana, Arkansas, where it met the rails of the Texas & Pacific.

Despite some early success, the Pacific Railroad was unable to keep up payments on its bonded debt, and in 1868, the state of Missouri foreclosed its lien on the property. Existing management continued to operate the Pacific under the supervision of a state railroad commissioner until mid-1872. At that time, the Pacific was leased for 999 years to the Atlantic & Pacific Railroad Company, a predecessor of the Frisco.

Within four years, however, the A&P itself was in default and the company was sold to an investors' group in New York. The Pacific was reincorporated as the Missouri Pacific Railway

Company in October, 1876. In 1879, controlling interest in the MoPac was purchased by financier Jay Gould. In that same year, he gained control of the Texas and Pacific.

During the next several years, the MoPac was consolidated with a number of subsidiaries and branch lines in Missouri, Nebraska and Kansas, each time retaining the Missouri Pacific name. In January, 1881, Jay Gould purchased controlling interest in the St. Louis, Iron Mountain & Southern. He then owned and operated both the Missouri Pacific and the Iron Mountain, but maintained separate corporate structures for the two roads.

Total integration would not come until 1917, twenty-five years after Jay Gould's death. By that time, the Iron Mountain's trackage had expanded from its original St. Louis-Texarkana route to include secondary lines and branches in Illinois, Arkansas, Tennessee and Louisiana.

In Texas, the Houston & Great Northern Railroad Company was chartered in 1866 to build a line from Houston to the Red River, on the Texas-Oklahoma Territory border. Four years later, the International Railroad was also organized to build from the Red River to the Rio Grande.

In 1873, the International and the H&GN were consolidated as the International & Great Northern. By that time, the two railroads had completed a line from Houston to Palestine, Texas. By 1881, the route had been extended to San Antonio and Laredo.

Also in the Lone Star State, the Texas & Pacific Railroad was incorporated in 1871 to build a railroad from Marshall, Texas to San Diego, California, via El Paso. Within ten years, the T&P had reached Sierra Blanca, Texas, 92 miles east of El Paso. There, construction gangs ran head-on into crews in the employ of Collis Huntington's Southern Pacific.

Given the temperament of the times, the stage was literally set for a shoot-out, averted only as a result of a court settlement reached in November, 1881 between Gould and Huntington. Under the terms of the agreement, the Texas & Pacific was granted operating rights over Southern Pacific into El Paso (and theoretically, but never used, all the way to Los Angeles). In return, the T&P agreed to discontinue further westward construction, and to relinquish any claims it had on land grants originally awarded to the Texas & Pacific but usurped by the SP. Thwarted in its bid for further westward expansion, the T&P turned east, completing a line from Marshall to New Orleans in 1882.

Like many railroads, the formative years of the Missouri Pacific were littered with countless defaults, reorganizations, bankruptcies and other financial highjinks. To name a few, the Missouri Pacific underwent reorganizations in 1868 and again in 1876, the I-GN in 1878, 1889 and 1908, the Missouri Pacific and the Iron Mountain in 1915, and the MoPac again in 1933. This last bankruptcy lasted until 1956, when, following the end of the trusteeship, the I-GN and Gulf

Coast Lines were formally merged into the parent company.

Other manipulations included the lease of the Missouri, Kansas & Texas (Katy) by the MoPac in 1880, the lease of the I-GN by the Katy in 1881 and the lease of the Wabash by the Iron Mountain in 1883. All these leases were set aside as a result of subsequent bankruptcies.

Between 1903 and 1905, the St. Louis, Brownsville & Mexico Railway, and the New Orleans, Texas & Mexico Railroad were chartered. These roads, along with several other short lines, were the predecessors of the combined Gulf Coast Lines, which were absorbed into the Missouri Pacific in 1925.

In that same year, the MoPac gained control of the International-Great Northern. This, along with several additional consolidations in Kansas, Colorado and Nebraska in 1909, and absorption of the Mississippi River & Bonne Terre in 1920 gave Missouri Pacific control of a railroad extending from St. Louis to Pueblo, Colorado in the west, and to Brownsville and Laredo, Texas in the south. MoPac also reached El Paso and New Orleans through its ownership of the T&P, and New Orleans again via the Gulf Coast Lines.

To the north, the Evansville & Illinois was chartered in 1849. As the successor Chicago, Danville & Vincennes Railroad, and later, the Chicago & Eastern Illinois, its rails eventually reached south from Chicago to Evansville and Mount Vernon, Indiana, and to Joppa and Thebes, in deepest southern Illinois. C&EI's entry into St. Louis was achieved at the turn of the century as a result of an agreement granting trackage rights over the Big Four Railroad (New York Central) southwest of Pana, Illinois. In 1902, C&EI came under the control of Benjamin Yoakum and the Frisco, and in 1903, the Rock Island.

C&EI entered bankruptcy in 1913, and was reorganized in 1920. Like MoPac, the road re-entered bankruptcy in 1933, emerging a second time in 1941. In 1967 the C&EI was jointly acquired by the Missouri Pacific and the Louisville & Nashville. MoPac gained possession of the lines from Chicago to St. Louis and Thebes; L&N took control of the route from Danville to Evansville, with shared ownership of the line between Danville and Chicago.

Final reorganizations took place in 1976, when the MoPac formally merged the C&EI and the Texas & Pacific Railroads into the greater Missouri Pacific, and in 1978, when the Missouri-Illinois and six other subsidiaries were also absorbed into the MoPac. On April 18, 1980, Missouri Pacific stockholders approved a merger with the Union Pacific Railroad. Under the terms of the merger, which was completed in 1982, the MoPac became a UP subsidiary. Although Missouri Pacific still exists in a legal sense (for tax reasons), its public identity has been all but washed away by the Armour Yellow and Harbor Mist Gray of the Union Pacific Railroad.

Below: One of the companion trains to the _Sunshine Special_ was _The Ozarker_, Trains 3-4. Here, the mostly-mail workhorse strikes a classic pose as she runs through south St. Louis at Morganford Road on a summer morning in the 1940's. _Joe Collias photo, Kevin EuDaly collection_

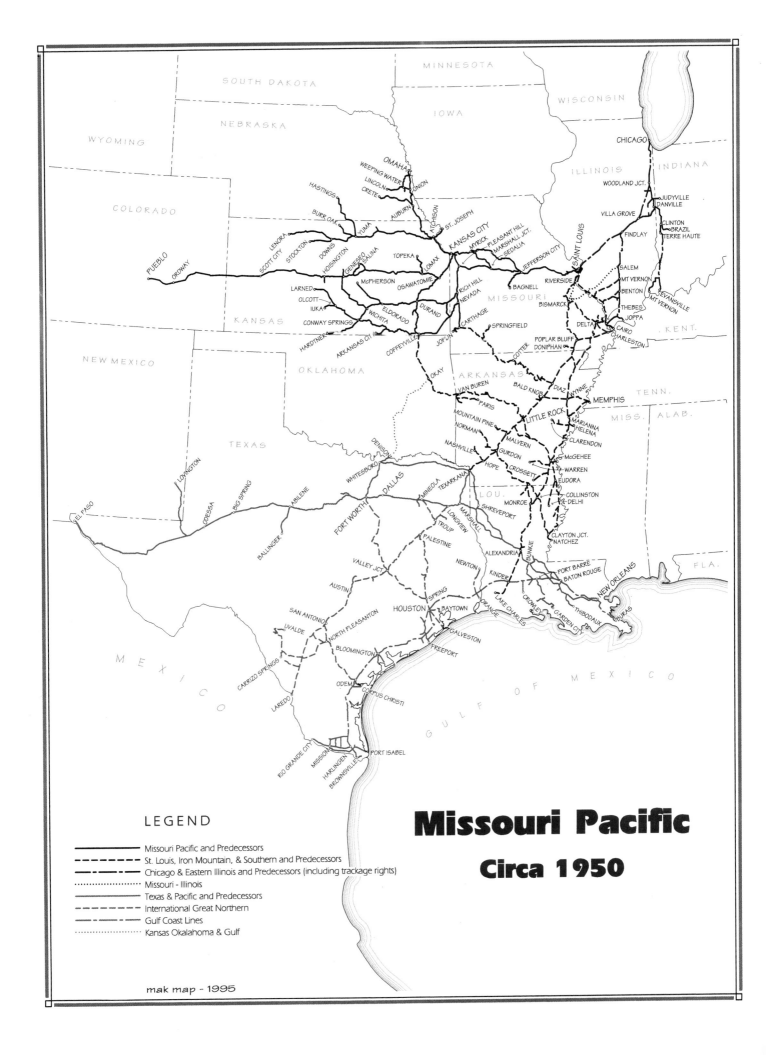

Missouri Pacific

Circa 1950

LEGEND

———————— Missouri Pacific and Predecessors
– – – – – – St. Louis, Iron Mountain, & Southern and Predecessors
–·–·–·– Chicago & Eastern Illinois and Predecessors (including trackage rights)
················ Missouri - Illinois
– – – – – Texas & Pacific and Predecessors
– – – – – International Great Northern
–·–·–·– Gulf Coast Lines
················ Kansas Okalahoma & Gulf

mak map - 1995

Though few likely recognized it at the time, America in 1940 stood balanced on the precipice of history. In Europe, following the near-disaster at Dunkirk, the Battle of Britain raged. Adolf Hitler's seemingly invincible Wehrmacht had overrun Poland, Belgium, Holland, Luxembourg, Denmark, Norway and much of France.

At home, despite strong isolationist sentiments, Congress passed the Selective Service Act, with the goal of inducting 800,000 draftees by the following July. In New York City, gangster Louis Lepke was sentenced to 30 years in prison for extortion, and more than 19 million people visited the World's Fair. The economic downturn that had started with the Crash of 1929 still touched most communities, as nearly 7 million Americans were without work.

Obituaries in 1940 included newspaper columnist Heywood Broun, former British Prime Minister Neville Chamberlain, auto giant Walter P. Chrysler and cowboy-actor Tom Mix. In the arts, William Saroyan won the Pulitzer Prize for drama with his play, *The Time of Your Life*. In sports, Cleveland's Bob Feller pitched an opening day no-hitter against the White Sox and, in

October, the Cincinnati Reds won the World Series by beating the Detroit Tigers four games to three.

In November, President Franklin D. Roosevelt defeated Indiana Republican Wendell Willkie for an unprecedented third term. And following a brutally difficult primary campaign, a little-known former judge from Jackson County, Missouri named Harry S. Truman was reelected to the United States Senate by a margin of 44,000 votes.

In the context of railroading, too, the world had begun turning slightly upside down. On gross revenues of more than $4 billion, the industry managed to net only a little more than $141 million. A third of the country's mileage languished in bankruptcy, including Rio Grande, Rock Island, Seaboard, North Western, Milwaukee, Frisco and Missouri Pacific.

In the south, what came to be recognized as the modern merger movement was born as Ike Tigrett's upstart Gulf, Mobile & Northern acquired the Mobile & Ohio to form the St. Louis-to-the-sea Gulf, Mobile & Ohio. In 1940, diesels were making inroads on the strength of EMD's FT quartet, numbered 103, that had barnstormed coast to coast the year before. And the

broad network of interurbans that blanketed the midwest was rapidly unraveling as Americans turned increasingly to the highways and the automobile as the preferred mode of transport from home to grandma's house.

Another change that had begun to radically alter the railroading landscape in this last year before total global war was the streamlined passenger train. Six years earlier, Burlington made history with the introduction of its revolutionary Zephyr on the route between Kansas City and Omaha. By 1940, streamlined passenger trains were operating in regular service on the Pennsylvania, New York Central, Milwaukee Road, North Western, Boston & Maine, Santa Fe, Union Pacific and others.

Below: The crew of *The Kay-See Flyer* seems anxious to get underway following their station stop at Jefferson City, Missouri on a pleasant afternoon in the late 1930's. The heavyweight *Flyer* and the Kansas City-Omaha *Marathon* were among the *Eagle's* predecessor daytime operations over the Omaha-to-St. Louis run. *Joe Collias collection*

Missouri Pacific
The Missouri River Eagle

mak map - 1995

MP's mechanical department specified that the new *Eagle* equipment be built "in the best, most substantial and workmanlike manner . . . all material must be of the best quality." This sequence of photos taken by ACF outside the St. Charles, Missouri plant shows the end result, including:

Middle left: mail-storage 700.

Bottom left: Baggage-mail car 710.

Top Right: 76-seat "standard" coach 720.

Middle right: 61-seat "deluxe" coach 730.

Bottom right: Diner-bar-lounge 740.

All ACF photos, Charlie Duckworth collection

Below: EMC E3 passenger units arrived on the MoPac on October 22, 1939, and immediately began a "breaking-in" on St. Louis-Kansas City locals 33 and 34. In December, 1939, spic-and-span E3 7001 simmers at Kansas City. Compare this view with a later view of this same unit shown on page 21. *Joe Collias collection*

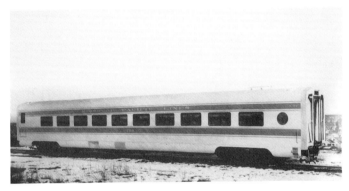

Above: Looking very much the way ACF and Mr. Loewy intended, the original six-car *Eagle* struts her stuff on the manicured right of way of the Eastern Division near Jefferson City. This obviously posed publicity photo was taken just prior to the beginning of revenue service on March 10, 1940. *ACF photo, Alan Wayne Hegler collection*

Below: Parlor-observation 750 brings up the tail end of the *Eagle* equipment at the American Car & Foundry facility in St. Charles, Missouri. Observation cars 750 and 751 were favorites of President Harry S. Truman in his travels after leaving office in 1953. Observation 750 now resides at the National Museum of Transport in St. Louis, where it is undergoing restoration. *ACF photo, Charlie Duckworth collection*

And so it was that on Sunday morning, March 10, 1940, the Missouri Pacific Railroad broke no new ground save its own with the maiden run of its all-new *Eagle* (the train did not become the *Missouri River Eagle* until the following year, when the impending arrival of the *Colorado Eagle* and *Delta Eagle* made the distinction necessary).

The first hint that streamliners were coming appeared in an article in the February, 1939 issue of the Missouri Pacific Lines Magazine. The article promised "Two Ultramodern Trains, each with 2,000 horsepower and six cars [that] will operate between St. Louis and Omaha on nine-hour schedules."

Two months later, contracts for two complete sets of equipment were let to American Car and Foundry in St. Charles, Missouri as ACF lot nos. 1880-1885. Delivery, planned for the fall of 1939, was finally completed in February, 1940.

As a result of studies of streamliners then in operation, the railroad determined that the new train would not be articulated, since a single bad-ordered car could sideline the entire consist. Accordingly, in addition to EMC E3 units 7000 and 7001, equipment for the new streamliners included mail storage cars 700-701, mail-baggage cars 710-711, 76-seat coaches 720-721, 61-seat "deluxe" coaches 730-731, diner-bar-lounge cars 740-741 and parlor-observation cars

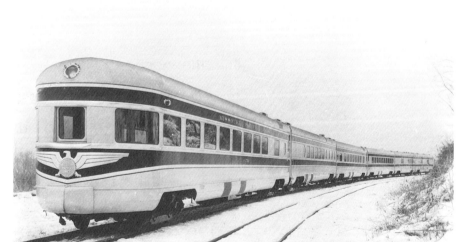

750-751. As it turned out, these were the only streamlined observation cars ever owned by the Missouri Pacific Railroad. Contrary to the common practice of many railroads at the time, the diners and parlor cars were not given names.

The name for the trains themselves was selected from among suggestions submitted by Missouri Pacific employees. A "name committee" was formed within the advertising department at MoPac's St. Louis headquarters to consider entries.

Company President L. W. Baldwin promised "...fame and the thanks of management to the Booster (employee) who comes forward with the best suggestion," which was to convey the ideas of "speed and bright moderness." It was further suggested that, whatever name was ultimately chosen, it would likely be carried forward to other streamliners that would follow.

The August, 1939 edition of the employee magazine announced that "The Eagle - swift, graceful, powerful and since the creation of our Republic, the symbol of American progress," had been selected as the name for the new train. In retrospect, the name must have been an obvious choice, since variations of it were put forth by fully a dozen employees among the several hundred who offered suggestions. Some of the ideas submitted included "Gray Eagle," "Eagle Scout," "Gold Eagle," and "Flying Eagle." Each of the winning contestants was invited by President Baldwin to be his guest on an early run of the new train.

Styling for the Eagle was developed by famed industrial designer Raymond Loewy, whose other credits included the Pennsylvania Railroad's GG-1 locomotive and 1938 Broadway Limited, and later, NASA's Skylab and Studebaker's last-gasp Avanti sports car. Exterior colors were light gray and a unique shade of blue, eventually called "Eagle Blue," accented with polished aluminum moldings above and below the pier panels and light cream stripes along the roof and bottom edge of the lower blue band. The cars were numbered and lettered "Missouri Pacific Lines" in aluminum.

The locomotives also carried the Eagle Blue livery, with silver and cream striping, gray roofs, side panels and pilots, and a gray "bow-wave" treatment sweeping back from the top of the anti-climber to blend into the lower panel on the baggage car. The cars were all equipped with full-width diaphragms, to simulate the look of a single unit.

Focal points of the exterior design were the stylized spread-winged eagles affixed to the nose of the locomotives and the rear of the observation cars. The observation's eagles were made of polished cast aluminum with MoPac's familiar red and white "buzzsaw" logo. The new Eagle's livery was striking, and with minor changes, served as the standard color scheme for all streamlined cars subsequently ordered by the railroad.

First to arrive on the property were the two E3's, which were accepted by the railroad in

October 1939. At the time they were delivered, the EMC staff boasted that the road crew could "wear a Palm Beach suit" while running the locomotive, thus making a point about the cleanliness of the diesel's cab compared to that of a steam engine. Photos taken at the time bear this out, as the crew was frequently shown wearing clean white coveralls.

The locomotives did not wait for the new streamlined cars, but were immediately put to work on Trains 33-34, the daylight locals operating between St. Louis and Kansas City over the River Subdivision through Boonville and Malden. By the time the new rolling stock began to arrive, the units were averaging nearly 7,500 miles a month in regular revenue service.

Below: Crescent, Missouri was a favorite photo site for Missouri Pacific devotees. Here, portholed E7 7005 leads a head-end heavy *Missouri River Eagle* toward Kansas City on March 19, 1952. Prominent in the consist are a homebuilt express-box, a turtle-roofed Pennsy express car and one of the new Planetarium dome coaches from Pullman-Standard. *Joe Collias*

Above: Here's westbound *Eagle* No. 5 running west on the double iron of MoPac's eastern division near Chamois, Missouri in the summer of 1940. Originally built as a single-track route, the line between St. Louis and Jefferson City was double-tracked in the 1920's at a cost of more than $15 million. *Charlie Duckworth collection*

Like most new streamlined trains under development at the time, the *Eagles* were designed to convey the feeling of comfort, quality and luxury. Indeed, ACF mechanical engineer Allen Clarke, upon learning that his company had been awarded the contract, was moved to enthuse that, "Keeping... within the realm of truth, I can say that these will be the most outstanding trains yet built." As if to underscore the point, General Specification Number One on each blueprint emphasized that "Cars must be built in the best, most substantial and workmanlike manner. All material must be of the best quality." In this, the railroad got its wish, as the first of the coaches were not retired for some 26 years. The diners lasted until 1965, and the observation cars were retired in 1962. The baggage and mail cars hung on even longer, remaining on the roster until 1967-69.

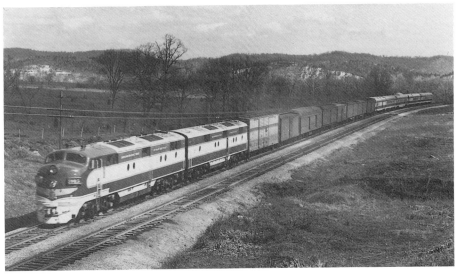

Above: Eastbound No. 106 rumbles into Atchison, Kansas on her way to Kansas City on the last day of November, 1947. Except for the parlor-observation bringing up the markers, none of the cars making up today's train are originals. The RPO is one of the two Budd cars purchased for the 1942 *Colorado Eagle*. The rest are heavyweights, modernized and repainted into the blue, cream and gray *Eagle* livery. *Harold K. Vollrath collection*

In contrast to the browns, grays and pale pastels used in passenger equipment in the mid-1960's, the 1940 *Eagle* cars were given interior treatments that were bright, tasteful and plush. Coaches were equipped with deep pile carpeting, reclining seats, Venetian blinds and individual window curtains. Interior colors for the coaches included mixed shades of blue and gray for the walls, yellow ceilings, and dark blue upholstery and carpeting. Bulkheads and blinds were finished in a silvery tone and the curtains were dark blue and mulberry.

Car illumination was provided by circular fixtures set into the ceiling, and by individual reading lights recessed into the overhead luggage racks. The women's lounge in the deluxe coach was decorated in blue grasscloth, pale blue and white floors, and wood rose-colored furniture. The men's lounge was decorated in more masculine hues of black, tan and wood tones. Each of the coaches measured 78 feet 9-5/8" over the end sills and 84 feet 6 inches coupler-to-coupler. Spacing between seats in both the standard and deluxe coaches was 42". Standard coaches seated 76. The deluxe cars accommodated 56, plus five in the lounges.

Diner-bar-lounges 740 and 741 contained a dining area for 24 and lounge seating for 20. The eating area was separated from the bar-lounge by a swinging door set into a bulkhead decorated with etched mirror panels. The ceiling was finished in a silver opalescent lacquer. Blue-gray was used on the sides, silver-rose on the drapes, rose-taupe on the upholstery, and wine red for the carpeting.

A special china pattern designed by Shenango China of New Castle, Pennsylvania featured an eagle flying alongside a streamlined Missouri Pacific train. International Silver designed special tableware embossed with an eagle and train logo. The hollow-ware and flatware were also given an "art-deco" treatment reflecting the streamlining of the train itself.

The lounge area included seating for sixteen in four booths, plus additional seating at two curved settees, each having small lounge tables. At the far end of the car was a bright blue semicircular bar decorated with lighted glass circles carved with the state flowers of the eleven states served by the railroad - an unusually forward-looking touch, since the *Eagle* itself operated in only three. A large mural behind the bar depicted an eagle in flight alongside the new train. The mural was widely reproduced and hung in many depots and traffic offices throughout the Missouri Pacific system.

The bar sections of cars 740-741 were decorated with gray carpeting, yellow leather upholstery and blue walls and draperies. Tabletops were pearl gray, and bar seats were a deep burgundy. Windows above the sofas were portholes rather than rectangular windows, and were designed to convey an atmosphere of intimacy and sophistication.

The kitchen was all stainless steel. The range burned oil, and refrigeration was generated by the water-ice method. An electric dish-

washer was built into one of the sinks at the side wall of the car. Ventilation was supplied by an exhaust blower over the range. Water was carried in two stainless steel tanks beneath the car and one overhead tank in the kitchen.

Parlor-observations 750 and 751 offered seating for 26 first-class passengers in revolving parlor chairs, plus an additional six in the observation end and five in the "stateroom" at the forward end of the car. In addition, the observation cars each included men's and women's toilets, plus baggage and linen lockers. Parlor seats were alternately upholstered in shades of brown and sea green. The ceilings were yellow and the walls apple green. The blinds and drapes were rose-beige and the carpeting was rose-mahogany. Like the coaches and dining cars, the observation cars measured 84 feet 6 inches over the coupler faces. By contrast, each of the head-end cars were 72 feet 10 inches coupler-to-coupler.

Promotional activities in support of the new trains kicked off four weeks prior to the first revenue runs. Various souvenir articles, including ink blotters and imprinted pencils proclaiming the *Eagle* the "World's Finest Streamlined Daylight Train" were distributed. In St. Louis, Missouri Governor Lloyd Stark joined the mayors of Omaha, St. Louis and Kansas City in a radio salute to the new train. Elsa Maxwell, known at the time as the "hostess with the mostest," donned engineer's cap, gloves and jump suit to mark the occasion. She later hosted a breakfast at Union Station to honor the railroad. The train was then placed on display at the Station for three days. On the first day alone, 25,000 people toured the train, including "Boost-

Below: Another view of grill-coach 873, with photos of the Colorado state capitol in Denver and San Antonio's Riverwalk decorating the bulkhead. Although the term "happy camper" had yet to be coined, this group seems to more than fit the bill. Note the Johnny Crawford look-alike in the window seat on the left. *ACF photo, Charlie Duckworth collection*

ers" from the company's headquarters, who were given the afternoon off expressly for that purpose.

Following the introductory ceremonies in St. Louis, the new train set off on a two-week tour of the Eastern Division so that on-line residents could inspect the railroad's pride and joy. In some towns, businesses were closed and schools recessed early to give factory and office workers and school children a chance to see the Eagle. A free round trip on the first run was won by the 100,000th person to visit the train while it was on exhibition in Omaha, and the oldest engineer in active service, J. F. Eppes, was given a cab ride on the maiden "flight." To demonstrate the free-rolling characteristics of the roller bearing-equipped locomotives, a professional wrestler named Maurice (The Angel) Tillet was hired to pull the locomotive along one of the station tracks for astonished onlookers.

Unlikely as all this may seem from the vantage point of the 1990's, it should be remembered that in 1940 the country was still struggling to throw off the lingering effects of the Depression. Under such circumstances, and in the absence of mass communications other than newspaper, newsreel and radio, the arrival of a colorful new streamlined passenger train was as exciting as the launching of a satellite or a moon landing would be to generations twenty or thirty years hence.

Once in actual revenue service, the $1.25 million streamliner pair ran on a daylight schedule between St. Louis and Kansas City, Missouri and Omaha, Nebraska, with connecting service

Above: Low-angle photography, a matched consist and the signal bridge with semaphore signal all contribute to the "classic" atmosphere of EMC E3 leading *The Eagle* near Jefferson City, Missouri in November, 1940. Note the brakeman hanging out the doorway of the observation car. *Harold K. Vollrath collection*

to Lincoln that, beginning in 1942 was provided by a unique motor train dubbed the *Eaglette*. Operating as Nos. 5-105 westbound and Nos. 106-6 eastbound, the *Eagle* was allowed five hours and five minutes for the 279 miles between Missouri's principal cities, and an additional three hours and fifty-five minutes for the 199 mile run to Omaha.

The *Eaglette* operated as trains 605-606, and ran between Lincoln and Union, Nebraska, where across-the-platform connections were made with the mainline trains. Running time for the forty-seven miles between Lincoln and Union was an unhurried one hour and twenty minutes.

Departures from St. Louis and Omaha were at 8:45am and 8:10am, respectively. Positive stops included Tower Grove, Jefferson City, Sedalia (home of ragtime composer Scott Joplin), and Warrensburg, the site of Central Missouri State College. Conditional stops included Kirkwood, California, Tipton, Holden, Pleasant Hill, Lee's Summit, and Independence.

North of Kansas City, the *Eagle* called at Leavenworth, Fort Leavenworth and Atchison, Kansas, and at Falls City, Nebraska City and Union, Nebraska, where the connection with trains 605-606 was made. Missouri Pacific Trailways buses met the *Eagle* at Atchison, Kansas to connect the mainline train with St. Joseph, Missouri. Motor coach service lasted until the mid-1950's, when the Saint Joe bus connection was dropped.

The train was an immediate success. At the end of its first six months, Eastern Division passenger revenues increased for all trains by 225% compared to the same period for 1939. Ridership on the *Eagles* had increased by 137% westbound and 165% eastbound since its introduction; the increase on the Omaha Division was 30%. It was projected by the Traffic Department that the increase was due to the public awareness generated by the new streamliners. On-time performance during the period was exemplary, with only one train in 26 running behind schedule.

Except for very minor adjustments, the schedule and running times of the *Eagle* stayed largely the same for the entire 31-year life of the train. Within weeks of its introduction, departure time from St. Louis was changed from 8:45am to 8:50am, to provide a more reliable connection with a Pennsylvania train from the east.

Following that change, departure time remained 8:50am until 1968, when it was pushed back to 9:30am. Arrival at Kansas City was 1:55pm. By 1948, this had been extended until 2:10pm, then 2:20pm in 1955 and 3:00pm in

Below: In 1948, MoPac took delivery of a large order of new streamlined cars from Pullman-Standard and American Car & Foundry. Posing aboard grill-coach 873 parked at the ACF yard in St. Charles, this trio of models enjoys coffee and a bottle of Coke while the porter chats amiably with his "passengers." *ACF photo, Charlie Duckworth collection*

1968, concurrent with the 9:30am departure. Arrival in Omaha was originally 6:05pm, then 6:40pm and finally 6:55pm. Changes in Omaha arrival times coincided with those made in the departure times described above.

Eastbound, departure from Omaha was 8:10am, changing to 8:00am in 1948. No further changes were made until shortly before the Omaha extension was discontinued in 1965, when it reverted to 7:00am. Arrival in Kansas City eastbound was 11:59am, with a 5:40pm arrival in St. Louis. This was advanced to 5:10pm in 1965, coincident with the earlier departure from Omaha, and remained unchanged thereafter until the service ended with the arrival of Amtrak.

The basic coach/parlor car/dining car configuration of the _Eagle_ stayed largely intact for the better part of the train's operating life, though not with precisely the same types of cars. During wartime, in response to the need for greater capacity, the _Eagle_ frequently operated with modernized and repainted standard cars. In later years, as additional streamlined cars arrived on the property, the original equipment set was broken up and the _Eagle_ ran with whatever appropriate equipment was on hand that particular day.

In 1948, MoPac received its first order of dome-coaches. Called "Planetarium Cars" by

the railroad, the domes were built by the Budd Company, of Red Lion, Pennsylvania, and were very similar in external appearance to Budd dome-coaches built for the Great Northern, Northern Pacific, and Wabash. The cars were numbered 890-892, with cars 890 and 891 lettered for the St. Louis-Denver _Colorado Eagle_. According to company records, the cars operated on at least an occasional basis on the _Missouri River Eagle_, but were not listed as part of the consist in public timetables of the era. Most likely, they were layover cars from Trains 11-12, and operated on a when-available basis.

In 1952, Missouri Pacific ordered a second batch of Planetarium Cars, this time from Pullman-Standard. These cars were somewhat different from the Budd cars, having lower dome profiles, no fluting and flat glass panels. The center panels were later covered over to reduce heat coming into the dome from the intense Texas sunshine. Although they were purchased four years later than the original Budd cars, the Pullman-Standard domes continued in the original number series as MP 893-896, with one additional car rostered as T&P 200.

Following the arrival of these cars, dome-coaches were shown as part of the _Missouri River Eagle_ consists in public timetables between 1953 and July, 1957. After that the domes were reassigned to the _Texas Eagles_ and did not

return to the _Missouri River Eagles_ until 1965. The upgrade proved to be short-lived, however. In 1967, the domes were withdrawn system-wide and, with one exception, sold to the Illinois Central for their _City of New Orleans_ and _City of Miami_ trains. The remaining car, no. 595 (nee 895) was dismantled at Sedalia by McCown Brothers, a local scrap dealer.

Parlor service continued in one form or another until 1967. The original parlor-observations ran between St. Louis and Omaha until June, 1961, when they were withdrawn from service and replaced by 30-seat full parlors. The round-ended cars did not operate again in revenue service. In 1962, 750 and 751 were formally retired; 750 was donated to the National

Museum of Transport in St. Louis, where it remains today. No. 751 suffered a more final fate, as it was cut up for scrap in Sedalia in that same year.

The full parlors, numbered 752-755, were not original Missouri Pacific cars, but were built by Pullman-Standard for the Chesapeake & Ohio in 1950. The cars were acquired by MoPac during a large scale sell-off of C&O equipment in 1959. The C&O parlors could be identified by their welded construction, absence of signature MoPac portholes, and by their fluted panels below the windows.

Like the railroad's earlier parlor cars, and despite having nameboards, the C&O cars were identified by number only during their tour of duty on the Missouri Pacific. 752-755 operated in parlor service on the *Missouri River Eagles* until 1963, when they were rebuilt into coaches 490-493.

First-class seating continued to be offered by a pair of parlor-diners, which were bumped by grill-coaches in February, 1967. After that, the only changes in the consists were the elimination of baggage and express cars in November of that same year. The trains then operated as two- or three-car coach/grill-coach consists powered by a single E-unit or boiler-equipped geep until their final runs in May, 1971.

During the 1940's and 1950's, the *Missouri River Eagles* were but a part of the railroad's passenger fleet operating over the Eastern Division. Mainline running mates included Nos. 9-10, the overnight *Missourians* to Kansas City; Nos. 11-12, the *Colorado Eagles* to Denver; Nos. 15-14, the afternoon mail and express trains to Kansas City; and Nos. 19-20, the overnight *Sunflower* to Omaha, Kansas City and Wichita.

Except for a handful of locals, including Nos. 35-36, MoPac's last two commuter trains, this was the lineup until 1954, when the *Sunflower* was discontinued. Although lightly patronized at the end, the trains' last runs did attract a great deal of publicity owing to their status as mainline operations. In fact, however, MoPac had been quietly pruning local passenger trains for years. Between 1948 and 1954, fully thirty-

Below: Heavyweight coaches and a substitute observation, or possibly one of the road's business cars, are in evidence as westbound No. 5 drifts through the MoPac shop town of Sedalia, Missouri. The date is February 1, 1948, and winter is holding full sway across the frozen Missouri heartland. *Joe Collias collection*

Above: In a scene that is quintessentially "railroady," the flagman of MoPac 15 checks his orders as passengers load on a chilly afternoon at Kirkwood in April, 1964. In its accustomed position on the markers end this day is ACF-built diner-lounge 38 (formerly 843). *Wayne Leeman photo, Joe Collias collection*

nine train pairs representing nearly 11,000 train-miles per day had been lopped off, including the *Eaglette* motor trains between Union and Lincoln.

Although full retreat was still a decade away on the Missouri Pacific, by the mid-1950's the handwriting was on the wall. In 1957, American railroads lost more than $723 million on passenger service based on the I.C.C. formula for full expense allocation, and $113.6 million on an out-of-pocket (direct expense) basis. MoPac itself dropped nearly $18 million based on the I.C.C. formula, although the true loss on an avoidable-cost basis was probably closer to $2 million.

Above: E8 7019 does the honors on May 29, 1959, as Train 110, the Omaha-Kansas City connection for the overnight *Missourian* begins its southbound jaunt. Incredibly, the little train will consume five hours and twenty minutes in covering the 199-mile run down the west bank of the Missouri River. *W. C. Whittaker collection, courtesy Ed Hawkins*

Right: What's a black switch engine doing in a book about blue and gray *Eagles*? Unlikliest members of the MoPac's passenger locomotive fleet were ugly-duckling NW4's 4102 and 4103. These 900 horsepower units were purchased from EMC in 1938 for switching duties around St. Louis Union Station. Here 4102 pauses between assignments at St. Louis in April, 1957. *Richard R. Wallin photo, Louis Marre collection*

Right: Companion trains to the *Missouri River Eagles* were nameless afternoon runs 15-14. Essentially daylight mail runs, the trains also included a consist that was every bit the equal of the *Eagle*, with coaches, a diner-lounge and a railroad-owned parlor car. In the mid-1950's, a 14-car No. 15 is caught raising the dust from freshly-ballasted track east of Valley Park, Missouri. The track at upper right is the Frisco main line between St. Louis and Oklahoma City. *Charlie Duckworth collection*

Right: E-units were the usual power for the *Missouri River Eagle*, but when they were in the shop, other power was available to pinch-hit. In September, 1948, steam generator-equipped F3 563 and a companion B-unit head up the *Eagle* at Omaha Union Station. *Charlie Duckworth collection*

Left: Infrequently photographed because of its midnight-to-dawn schedule, Train 10, the mostly-mail *Missourian* makes an easy 30 MPH as she rolls into St. Louis on May 7, 1947. That teakettle in the background looks like one of those high-speed 4-6-4's that powered Wabash's Kansas City-St. Louis passenger flyers. *Charlie Duckworth collection*

Competitors in Blue: MoPac and the Wabash

During the early 1900's, passengers traveling by rail between Kansas City and St. Louis had a wide choice of carriers, including Burlington, Wabash, Alton, Missouri Pacific, and Rock Island. By the 1950's, however, this once-competitive corridor was down to two direct routes: Wabash and MoPac.

A third route, Rock Island, saw its varnish dwindle down to a pair of locals between Kansas City and Eldon, Missouri, over what had become a rickety, 200-mile branch line. Rock Island's service was dropped altogether by the end of the decade, and the route became freight-only before being conveyed in inoperable condition to Cotton Belt in the early 1980's.

Below: A duo of Wabash E-units in old and new paint schemes backs Train 210, the *City of St. Louis* into the trainshed at St. Louis on May 23, 1962. During this period, the *City* handled sleepers and reserved-seat coaches between St. Louis and Los Angeles-San Francisco. Seat charge from the West Coast was $2, but no charge was added between St. Louis and Kansas City.
Roger Darling photo, TRRA Historical and Technical Society collection

Though lacking the scenic attractions of MoPac's river route, Wabash's feature trains across Missouri were good ones. Nos. 9-10, the *City of St. Louis*, was a classy joint operation with the Union Pacific. Dating from 1946, the *City* eventually offered domes, a full lounge, a diner, sleepers and coaches between St. Louis, Kansas City, Denver, Los Angeles, San Francisco and Portland.

Running mates for the *City* were Nos. 3-12, the *City of Kansas City*, and Nos. 17-18, the *Midnight Limited*. The *City of Kansas City* was a daylight streamliner introduced in 1947 that featured a diner-lounge, a parlor observation car, and later, domes; the overnighters were more standard fare that carried both 12-2 and 6-6 heavyweight sleepers.

On the run to Omaha, Wabash operated No. 11, the overnight *Omaha Limited/Des Moines Limited* between St. Louis, Nebraska and Iowa. Eastbound counterparts were night trains 14 and 18, the *St. Louis Limited*. MoPac had no direct service between St. Louis and Omaha and no routes at all in Iowa - perhaps no great disadvantage, since by 1961, the Wabash's Iowa-Omaha trains had become a combined mixed train between St. Louis and Council Bluffs. The *City of Kansas City* eventually lost its domes and parlors and degenerated into a head-end and coach operation similar to MoPac's 15-14. Both trains

died in the late 1960's at the hands of Wabash successor Norfolk & Western.

Daily service on the *City of St. Louis* was inaugurated on June 2, 1946. Unlike UP's other *City* streamliners, Nos. 9-10 were initially made up of two-tone gray cars in the *Overland* livery, rather than the yellow and gray used for the rest of the *City* fleet. At first, Wabash E7's ran as far west as Denver, and UP units operated into St. Louis. After a short time, however, Wabash began to complain about mileage equalization for its locomotives, and after that, each road's power remained on home rails.

In the beginning, the *City of St. Louis* did not actually operate all the way to the west coast, but terminated instead in Cheyenne, Wyoming, where the St. Louis-Los Angeles cars were combined with the consist of Train 1, the *Los Angeles Limited*. St. Louis-Portland cars were handed off to No. 11 at Green River. This was the operating pattern until 1951, when Nos. 9-10 finally did start running through from St. Louis to Los Angeles, with the Portland cars switched out at Green River. In 1964, as passenger traffic everywhere began to sink into terminal decline, the *City of St. Louis* and the *City of Los Angeles* were combined on the western end of their runs between Ogden and Los Angeles.

A typical consist for No. 9 in the early 1950's included baggage and mail cars between

St. Louis and Kansas City, St. Louis and Denver and Kansas City and Denver. In addition, the train handled coaches between St. Louis-Oakland, St. Louis-Portland, and St. Louis-Los Angeles, plus a dormitory-club and a full dining car between St. Louis-Los Angeles.

Sleepers included a 4-12 car between St. Louis-Los Angeles and 6-6-4 car between St. Louis-Portland, St. Louis-Oakland and Kansas City-Denver. One or more storage-mail cars were also occasionally attached to the rear of the train west of Denver. In addition, it was common for weekend runs to include at least one Wabash heavyweight coach between St. Louis and Kansas City to handle overflow local traffic. Customary length of the train was 10-13 cars.

During the period following Norfolk & Western's takeover of the Wabash in late 1964, the *City* operated out of St. Louis with a 6-6-4 *American*-series sleeper, a 10-6 *Pacific*-series sleeper, a dining car (yellow UP or a blue and silver ex-*Bluebird* or *City of Kansas City* car), a dome-coach, two or more straight coaches and a lengthy cut of mail and express cars.

Typical of all passenger operations involving Union Pacific, standards were high. The trains were run clean and on time, and the equipment was always in excellent condition. The author rode the *City* many times during the late 1960's, and cannot ever recall any equipment failures, bad food, or (except for one dining car waiter) surly service.

For the life of the train, UP and Wabash-N&W equipment alike ran all the way from St. Louis to the west coast. To maintain a uniform look for the train, several Wabash-N&W coaches, sleepers, and at least one dome-coach were painted in UP yellow and gray with scarlet lettering. Wabash diners and head-end equipment, however, remained resolutely blue.

After Wabash's E-units departed, motive power east of Kansas City was two or three

N&W passenger Geeps or Alco RS-11's, including ex-Wabash and Nickel Plate units. West of Kansas City, the Wabash diner was replaced by a UP car, a UP lounge was added, and UP motive power and head-end equipment replaced the N&W equipment. Departure from St. Louis was at 2:00pm with arrival in Kansas City 7:25pm. Kansas City-St. Louis running times were 10:50am-4:25pm.

Through the mid-1960's, the *City* did a reasonably healthy business, subject to the usual summertime-Christmas traffic fluctuations. During the holiday season, the train was routinely crowded with students from on-line colleges such as Kansas State University, the University of Kansas and the University of Missouri (connecting from Columbia, Missouri at Centralia via a one-car stub train) returning home for semester and Christmas break. Like other *City* trains, a reserved-seat charge was required on Trains 9-10.

Through west coast service over the Wabash/Norfolk & Western hung on until 1968, when the former Los Angeles-St. Louis coaches and sleepers were terminated in Kansas City, and the Union Pacific portion of the run was renamed the *City of Kansas City*. N&W continued to operate local Trains 209-210 between St. Louis and Kansas City with coaches and a diner-lounge, but without a dome or sleeper. Even in reduced form, the trains failed to come anywhere near covering their operating costs, and the N&W discontinued the train on April 17, 1969.

In spite of the gloomy prognosis (or perhaps because of it), General Passenger Traffic Manager R. J. McDermott wrote an article for the December, 1957 Missouri Pacific Lines Magazine entitled "Passenger Traffic Is Good Business... And We Want All Of It We Can Get!" In the article, Mr. McDermott reminded his readers that the MoPac would gross more than $28 million on passenger service for the year. Ominously, however, only $12 million would be generated by the railroad's 1.5 million revenue riders. The rest would come from the post office and from express customers.

In his pep talk, Mr. McDermott went on to say: "Let's be realistic - you know as well as I that too many of us have a defeatist attitude about the passenger business." In an "open letter" to Mr. McDermott published in that same article, MoPac Chairman Russell Dearmont added:

"It is hard for me to accept the views of many that the railroads should get out of the passenger business as fast as they can. I can't help [feeling] that if we would do more constructive thinking and less talking about quitting, we would find a way to improve the situation. I would like to have you and your associates in our passenger department give serious thought to improvements in our service that you think may encourage greater use of our trains."

One such idea, inaugurated in December, 1957, was the introduction of "Eagle Travel Tray Meals." These eat-at-your- seat, one-price meals were offered on all *Eagle* trains as a way to boost food service revenues. A sample breakfast menu included pork sausage, scrambled eggs, fried potatoes, toast or muffins, marmalade and a beverage for seventy-five cents. A sample lunch-dinner menu featured salisbury steak with onion sauce, potatoes and vegetable, bread and butter, a fruit cup, mint wafer and beverage for an even dollar.

The program was apparently a success, as more than 83,000 Travel Trays were served during 1958. After a couple of price increases in 1961, the program was finally dropped when the railroad began switching from dining cars to grill-coaches on many of its trains.

Another innovation offered on Eastern Division trains was the introduction of ten-ride tickets between Jefferson City, St. Louis and Kansas City. Under this program, frequent riders to and from the state capitol could purchase a ten-ride coupon for the price of eight, effectively a 20% discount. This promotion apparently was not too successful, however. With the exception of October, 1958, the first full month the program was in effect, the railroad averaged fewer than 40 coupon sales per month.

Other attempts to increase revenue included the availability of two roomettes for the price of a double bedroom, and weekend Christmas-season "Santa Claus Fares," which offered round-

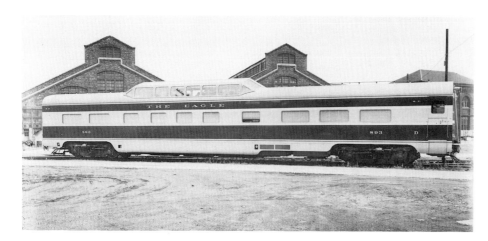

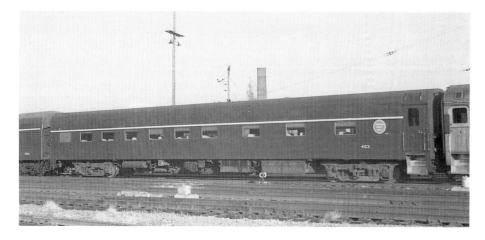

Top left: The final Planetarium dome-coaches delivered to the Missouri Pacific Lines were MP 893-896 and T&P 200. The cars were built by Pullman-Standard in 1952, and ran in *Texas Eagle* and *Missouri River Eagle* service until 1967. Shown here is no. 893, posed for her birthday picture outside the Pullman-Standard plant in Chicago. *Pullman-Standard photo, TRRA Historical and Technical Society collection*

Middle left: This is what happens when a coach is made out of a sleeping car. Coach 403 was built in 1948 by Pullman-Standard as 14-1-2 *Pullman Eagle Village*. The uneven window spacing resulting from the conversion must have made sight-seeing difficult for at least some of the riders. *Art Riordan photo, John Eagan collection*

Lower left: Box-express cars 135-184 were the answer to a what turned out to be a short-term need for head end equipment. Built by MoPac's DeSoto shops in 1962, the cars proved to be too low and too light for general freight service after passenger operations were cut back in the late 1960's. Many of the cars wound up their careers performing maintenance-of-way chores, or hauling lightweight commodities such as cotton or hay. *Art Riordan photo, John Eagan collection*

Below: Photographer Louis Marre calls this shot "The End of the Road." On October 8, 1961, EMD E3 7001 sits forlornly on a weedy siding at the MoPac shops in North Little Rock, Arkansas. More than 21 years after her shiny debut, she faces a bleak future at the business end of the scrapper's torch. *Louis Marre*

Above: Between 1952 and 1954, MoPac acquired 18 dual-service Alco FPA-2 locomotives. Numbered 361-373 and 388-392, these steam generator-equipped units most frequently found work on mail extras and holiday second sections of regularly scheduled trains. On a sunny January 3, 1953, FPA-2 372 leads an unidentified mate on a head-end heavy consist at California, Missouri. *Louis Marre collection*

trip travel for the price of a full-fare one-way ticket, with an additional charge of only twenty-five cents for children under the age of 12. Two "innovations" that probably didn't accomplish much were the imposition in 1960 of a service charge for checked baggage, and an increase in the charge to rent a pillow from twenty-five to thirty-five cents.

Despite the railroad's best efforts, passenger revenues continued to slide, and cost reduction began to replace service improvements as the order of the day. In 1962, a general renumbering of passenger trains took place. The *Missouri River Eagles* swapped their original 5-105-106-6 timetable numbers for Nos. 17 westbound and 16 eastbound between St. Louis and Omaha.

During that same year the railroad also began to take on a more austere overall appearance. Victims of a repainting program begun in 1961, the smart, Loewy-designed blue-and-gray livery quickly disappeared beneath a new coat of Dark Eagle Blue, more familiarly known as "Jenks blue," in dubious honor of new president Downing B. Jenks, who decreed the change.

Viewed by traditionalists as a retrograde step, the new hue nevertheless proved to be an economical choice. With relief provided only by white reflective tape and red MoPac heralds, Jenks blue became the standard motive power and passenger equipment color until Union Pacific washed it away with a flood of Armour Yellow and Harbor Mist Gray following the merger in 1982.

By 1966, in any shade of blue, the rout was on. In April, Trains 11-12, the once-proud *Colorado Eagles* ran their last miles between St. Louis and Pueblo. By then, it was a mercy killing. The trains had become an embarrassment two years earlier, when diner and Pullman service was dropped west of Kansas City and the train became a coach-only operation that rattled its way through the Kansas night to a crack-of-dawn connection with the Rio Grande.

Next to go were the overnight *Missourians*, which had lost their names during the May, 1962 renumbering. In December, 1966, the railroad withdrew the sleeping cars, ending all Pullman service over the route. The trains themselves continued to operate as Nos. 19-18 until 1968, when cutbacks by the Post Office Department wiped out the major portion of their revenue base and gave the railroad the excuse it needed to call it quits. The trains, which in better days often ran up to 40 cars long, made their final runs on November 1, taking with them the last overnight railroad passenger service of any kind between Kansas City and St. Louis.

Perhaps for sentimental reasons, retrenchment for the *Missouri River Eagle* was more

gradual. In February, 1963, the bus service that had replaced the *Eaglettes* between Lincoln and Union in 1954 was dropped. In December, 1963, the railroad petitioned the Missouri Public Service Commission for permission to discontinue the *Eagle* between St. Louis and Kansas City. The petition did not include the Omaha portion of the run, as the state of Missouri had no authority over service outside its own borders.

The PSC's response was pure political one-upmanship. Not only was the petition contested, but for good measure, the railroad's lawyers were also ordered to show cause why Missouri Pacific trains should not continue to serve the station at Tower Grove, even though the ticket office at the joint MoPac-Frisco facility had been closed in 1962.

Not surprisingly, the discontinuance petition was turned down. MoPac (and Frisco) were eventually able to claim a small victory when the Tower Grove station closed for good on September 11, 1964. Less than a week short of a year later, the *Missouri River Eagle* made its last run between Kansas City and Omaha, ending MoPac passenger service to Nebraska's largest city. After that, the *Eagle*, which retained her name to

Opposite page top left: E8 36 (ex-T&P 2016) powers coach 403 and grill-coach 563, the consist of St. Louis-bound Train 14, on April 19, 1968. The empty trainsheds of Kansas City Union Station are an indication of the state of passenger operations during the last years before Amtrak. *Larry Thomas*

Opposite page top right: The "Arrivals & Departures" board at Kirkwood pretty much sums up the state of MoPac passenger operations in July, 1970. Note that Nos. 15-14, nameless in public timetables since the early 1950's, have been dubbed the *Easterner* and *Westerner*. Perhaps Agent Weideman felt this small elevation in status would increase the customer appeal of the afternoon schedules. *Larry Thomas*

Above: Rising steam makes E7 14 look a little like the family clunker with a broken radiator hose as she pauses for a crew change, and to load mail and passengers at Jefferson City, Missouri. The date is December 4, 1965, and the abundance of power provided by the trio of E-units suggests that No. 16 is carrying a heavy load of holiday mail. That's the state capitol building visible above the classic "Jeff City" depot. *Louis Marre*

the end, operated between St. Louis and Kansas City only.

On Amtrak conveyance day, May 1, 1971, Trains 15-14 and 17-16 were the last passenger trains operating over the Eastern Division. Although service was initially provided by Amtrak's star-crossed New York-Kansas City *National Limited*, and later by the more successful *Ann Rutledge* and *St. Louis/Kansas City Mules*, an era had unmistakably passed. Following their

last arrivals at St. Louis and Kansas City Union Stations, a service tradition born in the shadow of Depression and war thirty-one years earlier came to an end.

Sample consist of Train No. 17, the *Missouri River Eagle* at Kansas City, Missouri, on September 18, 1965: MP E8's 41, 38; MP storage-mail 176; PRR storage-mail 2035; REX express 6393; PRR storage-mail 2015; MP railway post office 1015; T&P coach 475; MP coach 425; MP dome-coach 590; T&P diner-lounge 44.

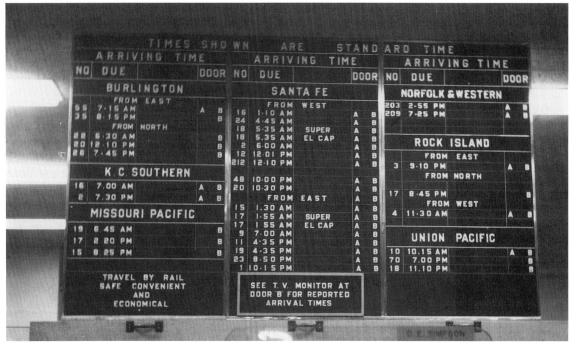

Above: Kansas City Union Station was still a reasonably busy place in the early part of 1968, as the Arrival Board above the ticket counter attests. Not counting Santa Fe's combined operations, no fewer than 32 trains still called at the big barn. A year later, however, the number of arrivals was down to 18, as all remaining operators reduced service in the wake of cutbacks in RPO operations by the Post Office. *Larry Thomas*

Opposite page bottom: Trailing mostly Penn Central equipment, but with a MoPac diner and a UP Pacific-series sleeper, Amtrak's westbound *National Limited* takes a breather at Jefferson City. The *National* was a New York-Kansas City operation, which accounts for the expanded consist. However, undependable timekeeping and skimpy ridership made the train an early casualty during the Carter administration's budget cuts. *Charlie Duckworth collection*

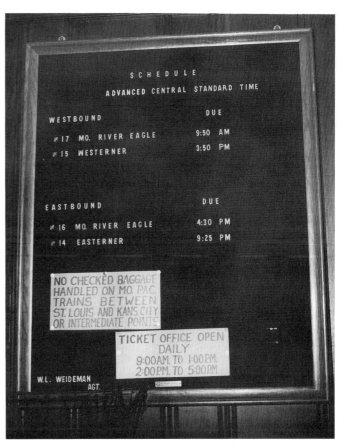

S C H E D U L E
ADVANCED CENTRAL STANDARD TIME

WESTBOUND	DUE
#17 MO. RIVER EAGLE	9:50 AM
#15 WESTERNER	3:50 PM

EASTBOUND	DUE
#16 MO. RIVER EAGLE	4:30 PM
#14 EASTERNER	9:25 PM

NO CHECKED BAGGAGE
HANDLED ON MO. PAC
TRAINS BETWEEN
ST. LOUIS AND KANS. CITY
OR INTERMEDIATE POINTS

TICKET OFFICE OPEN
DAILY
9:00AM. TO 1:00 P.M.
2:00 P.M. TO 5:00 P.M.

W.L. WEIDEMAN
AGT.

From the vantage point of Fortress America, the world by 1941 had become a very dangerous place. In Europe, the war was going badly, as Germany gained effective control of everything in the west between Poland and the Pyrenees. In the east, the Molotov-Ribbentrop Nonagression Pact proved to be no more than a scrap of paper when the Nazis turned on their erstwhile ally and, on June 22, invaded the Soviet Union.

In the Pacific, the Japanese encountered no effective resistance in their drive to seize control of virtually all of southeast Asia. For America, the question was no longer if, but when, we would become an active participant. The answer would come on an early Sunday morning in December, at a place called Pearl Harbor.

With the onset of war, Americans were confronted overnight with a number of unfamiliar rules and regulations, including gasoline, meat and sugar rationing, nighttime blackouts in coastal cities and curbs on business and recreational travel. Restrictions on the use of raw materials and heavy machinery were imposed

Missouri Pacific
The Colorado Eagle and connections

Below: E7 7009 eases to a stop at the depot in Kirkwood, Missouri with the eastbound *Colorado Eagle*, train No. 12, in August, 1954. The train's consist this day is unusual in that the first four cars are all Railway Post Office cars. Only the two mainline tracks remain at the depot today. *Joe Collias*

Left: Just a week after her debut, EMD E6 7002 and companion E6B 7002B power seven cars of the *Colorado Eagle* at an easy 55 MPH through Wolhurst, Colorado. The track is the joint line of the Rio Grande and the Santa Fe, making the *Eagle* at this point a D&RGW operation. *Preston George photo, John Wegner collection*

Right top: The first streamlined sleeping cars to be regularly assigned to a Missouri Pacific passenger train were the four 6-6-4 cars delivered in 1942. Named *Arkansas River*, *Colorado River*, *Eagle River*, and *Gunnison River*, the cars performed yeoman duty for the MoPac until they were finally retired in 1967. Here, *Colorado River* poses for its official photo outside the Pullman works in May, 1942. *Smithsonian Institution photo, Alan Wayne Hegler collection*

Right middle: Budd-built dining cars *Cheyenne Mountain* and *San Isabel* were the only non-sleeping cars on the Missouri Pacific to be named. Those porthole windows were a MoPac signature feature, appearing on a wide variety of streamlined passenger cars as well as early E-series locomotives. *R. T. Dooner photo, Alan Wayne Hegler collection*

Above: Dormitory-grill-coach 723 underwent several rebuildings, first into a dormitory-coach and in 1965 into straight coach 425. The 1942 Budd product was removed from the roster and sold to Rail Leasing Corporation in 1968. The roofs of the 1942 Budd cars were not painted, but left in natural stainless steel. *Charlie Duckworth collection*

Below: Several 6300-series heavyweight coaches were rebuilt and modernized as "deluxe" coaches in the 1940's for service on the *Colorado Eagle*, *Sunflower*, and other MoPac trains. Here's coach 6309, repainted in the blue and gray *Eagle* livery with thermopane windows, air conditioning and portholed inserts in the vestibule doors. *Charlie Duckworth collection*

Below left: Three 8-1-3 heavyweight sleepers in the *Tower*-series were rebuilt in 1941 for *Colorado Eagle* service between Wichita and Denver. Here, *Temple Tower* is shown outside the Pullman shops in September, 1941. The others: *Shrine Tower* and *Beacon Tower*. *Smithsonian Institution photo, Alan Wayne Hegler collection*

by a government agency known as the War Production Board.

Within months, limitations were placed on, among other things, the manufacture of tires, civilian automobiles, and streamlined railroad passenger equipment. It was as a result of these restrictions that trains such as the *Panama Limited* and the *Colorado Eagle* were very nearly never built.

As it turned out, completion was finally permitted in order to allow the release of predecessor equipment for troop-train service. It is only for this reason that the story of the *Colorado Eagle* begins in the last months of peacetime instead of the first years of what became known as the Atomic Age.

Right: Though never a major operator of observation cars, Missouri Pacific did indulge in some colorful and occasionally creative tail signs. In this sequence, parlor 10610 displays two signs used on the *Royal Gorge* in 1947. The metal sign used a green background, red "buzzsaw," black lettering, and a yellow band. The illuminated drumhead had a red logo and lettering on a white background. The painting of the Royal Gorge was in green and brown with black accents. *Both Charlie Duckworth collection*

Below: Brand-new E8 7020 leads E7B 7010B and PA-3 8019 on the point of MoPac 11, the *Colorado Eagle*, through Maplewood, Missouri on a hazy afternoon in August, 1950. Until the end of service in 1961, the depot at Maplewood served MoPac commuter trains in and out of St. Louis Union Station. *Joe Collias collection*

Above: Before the *Colorado Eagle*, there was the *Scenic Limited*, a heavyweight deluxe flyer between St. Louis and the west coast. In this photo, westbound No. 11 rounds the curve at Kirkwood, Missouri. In another minute, she'll be braking to a stop at the classic depot. *Joe Collias collection*

In the summer of 1941, the Missouri Pacific Railroad fielded two pairs of steam-powered, heavyweight trains between St. Louis and the far west. The premier trains on the route were Nos. 11 and 12, the *Scenic Limited*.

The *Scenic*, which began through service in December, 1915, featured coaches, sleepers, dining and lounge service between St. Louis and Denver. Pullman accommodations included standard 10-1-2 and 16-section tourist cars to Denver and Salt Lake City. Also in the consist was a rather unlikely Little Rock-Denver Pullman that operated through Wichita, and connected with the mainline train at Geneseo, Kansas. For the economy-minded, or those simply less inclined toward culinary elegance, grill-coach meals were available between St. Louis and Pueblo, Colorado. Coach and Pullman connections for Salt Lake City and San Francisco via the Rio Grande and Western Pacific were made at Denver.

Westbound, the *Scenic* departed St. Louis at 1:45pm, with arrival in Denver at 8:45am the following morning. Eastbound, the train rolled out of Denver at 3:40pm and arrived at St. Louis at 1:15pm the next afternoon.

The other trains on the route were not really a paired operation, and offered uninterrupted service on the westbound leg only. Number 15, which was known as the *Royal Gorge*, included coach and sleeping car accommodations between St. Louis and Pueblo, where it connected with Rio Grande No. 1 for the remaining 120 miles into Denver.

In addition, the *Gorge* carried a parlor car, a diner-lounge and deluxe coaches between St. Louis and Kansas City, and an every-other-day sleeper for Los Angeles by way of a connection at Kansas City with Rock Island-Southern Pacific's *Imperial*. The L.A. sleeper made its return to St. Louis in the consist of the overnight *Missourian*.

Eastbound, unnamed No. 16 operated between Pueblo and Kansas City only, and offered a 10-1-2 sleeper and grill coach service. At Kansas City the train connected with No. 12 for the remainder of the trip to St. Louis, this despite having departed Pueblo two and a half hours ahead of the *Scenic*.

Flushed with the success of the original *Eagle*, and with the *Delta Eagle* cars already in production, MoPac elected to raise the ante one more time. According to the February, 1941 edition of the *Missouri Pacific Lines Magazine*, the railroad planned to order two complete train sets consisting of two sleeping cars, two coaches, a diner-bar-lounge, a mail-baggage car and an express car.

The new train was scheduled to cover the 1,021 miles between St. Louis and Denver in sixteen hours and five minutes, for an average speed of better than a mile a minute. Obviously, even for a depression-torn railroad strapped for cash, seven cars would seem to be a somewhat abbreviated consist for an overnight operation of a thousand miles. It would suggest that, despite the eventual release of the *Scenic's* heavyweight cars to the military pool, MoPac's original idea may have been for the new *Eagle* to operate as a premium service running in addition to, rather than instead of, the *Scenic* and the *Gorge*.

The article went on to say that "Each train will be powered by a 4,000 horse-power Diesel electric locomotive." This was due to the "size and speed requirements" of the train, and also the need to handle additional cars "if and when

the need arises." Apparently, there was some question what these locomotives would be:

"The forward unit will, of course, be streamlined and contain space for the engineer and fireman. The No. 2 unit [has] yet to be decided. This may be, in effect, a duplicate of the No. 1 unit, capable of being operated independently or in conjunction with the forward unit. Or it may be a dependent unit, lacking a cab and tapered head-end."

Plans called for a mid-afternoon departure from St. Louis with an early morning arrival in Denver, and for a late afternoon departure from Denver with a mid-day arrival in St. Louis. The apparent rationale for upgrading the Colorado service ahead of the Texas trains was the success of the *Scenic*.

According to Missouri Pacific publicists, the *Scenic* offered such outstanding scenic attractions that, even with standard cars and steam power, it was able to compete with the new streamliners operating over the Burlington and North Western-Union Pacific-Southern Pacific. Just where this scenery might be was not clear, however.

The trains were essentially overnighters and, except for the run along the Missouri River and a brief glimpse of the front range of the Rockies north of Pueblo, the best scenery on the routes traversed by the *Limited* and its competi-

tors were west of Denver, where the new *Eagles* were never destined to fly.

Though there was no indication that a name had yet been chosen for the new train, there was no doubt about what it would look like: "As now planned, the cars will be interchangeable with those of the *Eagle* and the *Delta Eagle*, being finished with twin bands of polished metal and in gray and blue color schemes."

Specifications for use by car builders in formulating bids were once again headed by the requirement that "cars must be built in the best, most substantial and workmanlike manner."

Despite the desire to match the earlier trains, however, it was not American Car & Foundry, which built the original *Eagle*, nor St. Louis Car Company, which was building the *Delta Eagle*, that got the contract. Instead, the coaches, diners and head-end cars were built in Hunting Park, Pennsylvania by the E. G. Budd Company. The sleepers, the first such streamlined cars to operate in the regular consist of a Missouri Pacific passenger train, were built by Pullman-Standard.

The 1941 Budd order included builder lots 96313-96317 and consisted of 11 cars numbered in the 700-series begun with the original *Eagle*. The Budd cars as delivered were baggage cars 702-704, baggage-mail 712-713, dormitory-coaches 722-723, 56-seat deluxe coaches 733-734 and diner-lounges 742-743. Unlike the original *Eagle* diners, these cars came with

names, *Cheyenne Mountain* (742) and *San Isabel* (743). They were the only streamlined non-sleeping cars on the Missouri Pacific ever to be named.

All the Budd cars were built from stainless steel using Budd's patented shotwelding technique. The exteriors had the same fluted panels as the company's other offerings, which had been built for the Burlington and other roads. However, except for the roofs, which were left unpainted, the *Eagle* equipment was not finished in natural stainless steel, but was painted Eagle Blue and gray following an acid-bath "pickling" process that enabled paint to adhere to the otherwise smooth surface.

As delivered, the new cars were lettered "Colorado Eagle" rather than the customary "Missouri Pacific Lines." Except for dome coaches 890-891, these were the only Missouri Pacific passenger cars lettered with a specific train name, as subsequent equipment carried "The Eagle" name only. Interiors for the Budd cars were styled by Henry Dreyfuss, designer of the 1938 streamlined version of New York Central's *Twentieth Century Limited*.

Sleeping cars for the *Colorado Eagle* were of the 6-6-4 (six section, six roomette, four double bedroom) type and were named for rivers in the state of Colorado, including *Arkansas River*, *Colorado River*, *Eagle River*, and *Gunnison River*. In an era that had already seen the beginnings of a movement toward all-room

cars, open-section sleeping cars were still being placed in service. This was because, at the time, government employees traveling on business were only reimbursed for the cost of a section.

The cars were delivered in 1942 and were operated under contract by Pullman crews, because of that company's rule that Pullman conductors and porters could only staff Pullman-built equipment. That requirement would be found by the courts in 1947 to be in restraint of trade, but in 1942, no railroad was anxious to take on the mighty Pullman Company. Missouri Pacific finally purchased the cars outright in 1945.

Eventually, the railroad was able to resolve its misgivings about motive power for the new *Eagles*. As in 1939, MoPac turned to Electro-Motive, this time for E6A units 7002-7003 and E6B boosters 7002B and 7003B. These were basically off-the-shelf production units except

Below: June, 1944 finds E3 7003 on the point of the *Colorado Eagle* at Jefferson City, Missouri. June also finds Allied forces storming the beaches at Normandy as No. 12 calls at Jeff City. Ahead: FDR's fourth, the liberation of Paris, President Truman, "Enola Gay" and finally, thankfully, peace. *Harold K. Vollrath collection*

Commuting on the MoPac

During the late 1890's, both Missouri Pacific and the Iron Mountain operated extensive suburban services in the St. Louis area. On the MoPac proper, these trains traced their origins to "accommodations" that began running on the Pacific Railroad between St. Louis and Kirkwood in 1873.

Suburban service on the Iron Mountain dated from 1889, when the Oak Hill branch opened between Tower Grove and Carondelet. The new line provided access into St. Louis Union Depot for the trains of the Iron Mountain and the Mississippi River & Bonne Terre, whose rails joined those of the Iron Mountain at Riverside Junction, 25 miles south of St. Louis. The MR&BT was chartered in 1888 as a subsidiary of the St. Joseph Lead Company.

By 1890, it had laid 33 miles of narrow-gauge track between Bonne Terre and Riverside. The track was relaid to standard gauge in 1893-94, during which time a final 14-mile extension to Doe Run was built. The line served as a freight and passenger link between St. Louis and St. Joe Lead's headquarters in Missouri's "Lead Belt" region. As late as 1929, the MR&BT ran four trains a day between Bonne Terre and St. Louis.

System-wide, Missouri Pacific commuter operations reached their high water mark in the period immediately prior to the turn of the century. According to the June, 1896 timetable, MoPac ran 10 daily and three weekend trains between St. Louis and Kirkwood, with two trains continuing west to Washington. In addition, eight weekday and 15 Sunday trains split off the main line at Lake Junction for the 12-mile run to Creve Coeur Lake, a popular recreation spot at the time. Iron Mountain service consisted of six Carondelet-St. Louis trains and eight St. Louis-Arcadia runs.

In 1896, MoPac also ran 14 trains between Pleasant Hill and Kansas City, and two trains between Omaha and Portal, Nebraska. Changes were on the way, however.

The June, 1917 timetable listed thirteen daily and three weekend trains between Union Station and Kirkwood, with three trains continuing west to Pacific and Washington. Tellingly, however, service to Creve Coeur Lake had been reduced to two weekday and three Sunday runs. Kansas City and Omaha-area suburban service had disappeared altogether.

Also by 1917, the Iron Mountain had eliminated commuter service south of DeSoto, and by the late 1920's, was out of the business. The MR&BT also dropped passenger service in 1929, and shortly thereafter was absorbed by the Missouri-Illinois, another MP subsidiary.

As local roads and highways improved during the next decade, suburban service on all St. Louis-area railroads dwindled to a bare minimum. By 1929, MoPac was down to six weekday and two weekend trains between St. Louis and Kirkwood.

Service on the competing Frisco was even more limited, with only three weekday and one weekend train operating between St. Louis and Valley Park. Frisco exited the commuter business altogether in 1933. Wabash ran a single train, known locally as "The Comm," between St. Charles and the Eads Bridge station in St. Louis. Like Frisco's offerings, The Comm expired in 1933.

Missouri Pacific's remaining service stayed more or less intact until July 22, 1940, when a fire inside the Union Station control tower forced the elimination of all suburban trains except for a pair of Labadie-Pacific-St. Louis locals that lingered into the 1960's. By that time, Trains 35-36, known informally as the "Pacific Eagles", had become minor celebrities as the only regular commuter trains in operation between Chicago and San Francisco.

According to the June, 1957 timetable, Train 36 departed Pacific at 5:20am and arrived in downtown St. Louis at 6:57am. Stops along the way included Eureka, Jedburg, Valley Park, Kirkwood, Webster Groves, Maplewood and

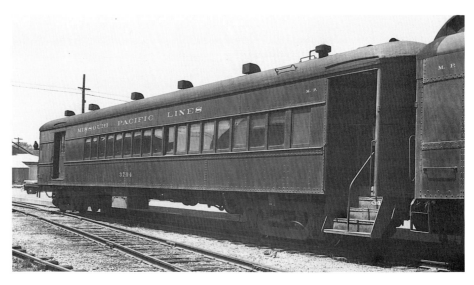

Above: The wide vestibule and low roofline betray car 3704's origin as a suburban car that formerly worked the line between St. Louis and Pacific, Missouri. The suburbs are a long way off today, as 3704 works regular passenger service at Arkansas City, Kansas. Wonder if MoPac shops left those 3-2 commuter seats in place! *Charlie Duckworth collection*

Left: Following a fire at the Union Station control tower in July, 1940, Missouri Pacific commuter operations were cut back to a single round trip between Pacific and St. Louis. In this photo, nearly-new FPA-2 372 leads No. 36 past a freight at Knox Avenue on the morning of March 19, 1953. *Charlie Duckworth collection*

Tower Grove. On the return trip, No. 35 departed St. Louis at 4:25pm and arrived back in Pacific at 5:50pm.

Obviously, the schedule was not constructed around the traditional "9 to 5" workday, but was designed to accommodate employees of the railroad itself, many of whom used the "Eagle" on a regular basis. Interestingly, no MP passes were accepted on the commuters, and there were no multi-ride tickets. Employees and non-employees paid the same fare, about forty-five cents from Kirkwood.

The "Pacific Eagles" made their final runs on December 15, 1961. By that time, patronage was down to a loyal core of slightly more than 200 regular riders, plus several hundred more "foul weather friends" who used the trains when

weather conditions turned sour, or during the occasional transit strike. According to employee-passenger Frank Bryan, the morning trip

Above: Early dieselization of commuter trains was obviously not a high priority on the MoPac. On September 25, 1951, light Pacific 6425 powers westbound Train 35 through a curve near Kirkwood. *Joe Collias photo, Kevin EuDaly collection*

Right: Until Amtrak showed up with its bi-directional RTG's, MoPac suburban trains were the only trains to enter St. Louis Union Station "head first" (all others backed in). In this very special photo taken on October 1, 1955 the author's late father, Gordon Stout (wearing a dark jacket and bow tie, near Alco FPA-2 388's cab ladder), hurries along the platform with a crowd of office-bound commuters just off "Pacific Eagle" 34 from Pacific, Kirkwood and Webster Groves. *Wayne Leeman photo, Joe Collias collection*

Commuting on the MoPac

was uneventful, except for being a little more crowded than usual.

In a radio interview at Union Station, the conductor admitted to having the best job on the railroad, a day's pay for each round trip. Festivities took place on the last outbound run, including an open bar for the regulars, black crepe on the outsides of the cars, an uncomfortable-looking Passenger Traffic Manager H. E. Mack, who accompanied the trip, and a slightly inebriated, trumpet-playing passenger who got off and blew taps at every stop out to Kirkwood.

An interesting "almost was" took place in 1956, when MoPac, the Terminal Railroad Association of St. Louis (TRRA) and the St. Louis Chamber of Commerce participated in a joint study to explore the possibility of expanding commuter rail service in the metropolitan area. Under the terms of the proposal, seven Budd Rail Diesel Cars (RDC's) were to be acquired. Service would consist of

six morning and three afternoon trains between Kirkwood and St. Louis, and three morning and six afternoon trains between St. Louis and Kirkwood.

The downtown terminus would not be Union Station, but a new depot that would be constructed at Eighth and Olive Streets, nearer the center of the business district. Trackage utilized would be the TRRA tracks in the tunnel that connected Union Station with Eads Bridge.

According to the proposal, the project would require nearly $3 million in capital expenditures, including $1.2 million for the RDC's, $500,000 to construct the Eighth and Olive station, $323,000 to extend the CTC system and the rest for track improvements, including the construction of crossovers inside the tunnel. It was anticipated that an additional $513,000 would be needed annually to operate the system.

Based on a 25-cent fare and a daily ridership of approximately 2,100 passengers, the system was projected to lose more than $377,000 a year. In addition, given that the RDC's would tie up the tunnel for three hours every morning and again every afternoon, a reroute of Pennsylvania, New York Central and Baltimore & Ohio

trains from the Eads to the MacArthur Bridge would have been necessary during those periods.

Drawing upon the available data, the Joint Committee was forced to conclude that the operation would be uneconomic on all fronts, and could not be justified. As a result, the opportunity to see *Eagle* colors applied to a small fleet of RDC's was lost, except, perhaps on the layouts of a few visionary model railroaders.

Below: The MoPac depot at Kirkwood, Missouri, shown here in April, 1970, dates from 1893. As built, the station included a 50-foot covered platform on the east (right) side, but this was removed following the cancellation of all but one of the suburban trains serving St. Louis. In the 1950's, Kirkwood hosted an even dozen arrivals and departures, including commuter trains 35-36. *Joe Collias*

for the signature portholes that were once again specified in place of standard rectangular windows.

As promised, the *Colorado Eagle* equipment was finished in the blue and gray scheme with silver and cream striping, though with variations from the original *Eagle* livery. The gray "bow wave" accent stripe no longer extended the full length of the unit, but ended instead in a reverse point just behind the cab steps.

A further departure was the blue paint applied to the pilots instead of the previous gray. Finally, although the Rio Grande had no financial interest in the train, the names of both railroads appeared beneath the wings of the aluminum eagle on the noses of the "A" units. The "buzz-saw" logo carried the train name in place of the usual "Missouri Pacific Lines" script.

Interestingly, in photos shot by Rio Grande's publicity staff, the prints were often retouched so that the "Rio Grande" name appeared on the engineer's side rather than the fireman's side, suggesting that D&RGW, and not MoPac, owned the train. The issue became moot when the locomotives were later repainted minus the train

Below: A favorite location for MoPac to showcase its candy trains was on the double-tracked portion of the Eastern Division between St. Louis and Jefferson City. In this scene to warm a publicist's heart, E7 7015 leads westbound No. 11 with two Planetarium dome coaches in the early 1950's. *Missouri Pacific photo, Charlie Duckworth collection*

Above: During the 1940's, the *Royal Gorge* was a reasonably plush MoPac-Rio Grande operation between St. Louis and Denver, with connections at Kansas City for the west coast. Shortly after the date of this photo in January, 1950, the *Gorge* was cut back to a St. Louis-Hoisington, Kansas job with a diner and parlor car that ran as far as Kansas City. *Otto Perry photo, Charlie Duckworth collection*

Above: There's a little bit of everything in this June, 1948 view of the *Colorado Eagle*, shown skirting the south bank of the Missouri River near Hermann, Missouri. In addition to the 1942 Budd cars, this day's No. 11 includes an ACF coach from the original *Eagle*, a 6-6-4 River-series Pullman, and a modernized heavyweight coach. And domes are only days away! *Joe Collias*

names. This was done after the E6's began to appear in service on other routes and a standardized paint scheme became necessary.

Exterior treatment for the rolling stock was also slightly different from the 1940 design. Most noticeably, the blue band below the windows was widened so that it extended all the way down to the skid rail above the skirting. Additionally, the sleeper roofs were painted in a darker shade of gray than that applied to the pier

panels. This second version of the *Eagle* livery became the final exterior paint scheme until the application of Jenks blue in the early 1960's.

The first run of the *Colorado Eagles* took place on June 21, 1942. In keeping with an agreement between the railroads and the United States government not to promote or otherwise create additional demand for rail travel, there was no publicity campaign for the new train. Recall that this was a time when every train

Right: Spanking-new 70-seat (46 down, 24 up) Planetarium dome coach 891 basks in the sunshine following delivery to the MoPac in the spring of 1948. Along with sisters 890 and 892, the Budd domes were the first three of eight dome coaches eventually owned by the road. The remaining cars were built by Pullman-Standard for *Texas* and *Missouri River Eagle* service in 1952. *Missouri Pacific photo, Alan Wayne Hegler collection*

station, bus depot and airport was papered with signs asking "Is This Trip Necessary?" Nevertheless, the train was an immediate success.

Once in daily operation, the *Colorado Eagles* ran as Nos. 11 and 12, effectively replacing the *Scenic Limited*, whose equipment was released for service in the military pool. The *Colorado Eagle* departed St. Louis at 4:15pm with a 9:15pm arrival in Kansas City. Positive stops enroute included Tower Grove, Jefferson City and Sedalia. Conditional stops were Webster Groves, Kirkwood, Washington, California, Warrensburg, Pleasant Hill and Independence.

The Eagle departed Kansas City at 9:25pm, using the tracks of the Kansas City Terminal to Tower 4, and then the Frisco line to Paola, Kansas (also used by the Katy). This arrangement saved 10 miles over the MoPac's own route between Paola and Kansas City. By 1961, however, shortly before the *Eagle's* downgrading, the route was changed to all-MP, so that No. 12 actually departed eastward before turning southwest at Sheffield Junction.

Positive and conditional stops on the way to Denver included Osawatomie, Herington, Lindsborg, Geneseo, Hoisington and Horace, Kansas, and Eads and Pueblo, Colorado. North of Pueblo, the *Colorado Eagle* operated over the joint track of the Rio Grande and the Santa Fe. Running as Rio Grande No. 3, the *Eagle* arrived in Denver at 9:30am following an intermediate stop at Colorado Springs.

Northbound, the *Eagle* used the Santa Fe's depot; southbound stops were at the joint Rio Grande-Rock Island station. Actual running time: 18 hours, 15 minutes; 2 hours and 10 minutes slower than originally planned. Eastbound, the *Eagle* departed Denver at 4:45pm and arrived at Kansas City at 6:45am. Arrival in St. Louis was at 12:15pm.

At Geneseo, Kansas, the train picked up the Wichita-Denver sleeper, which was forwarded in the consist of Trains 411-412. The Wichita-Geneseo locals consisted of one or more headend cars, a coach and a rebuilt heavyweight 8-1-3 sleeper. The heavyweights hung on until 1952 when they were replaced with the 1941-built 6-6-4's, which were displaced from the mainline train by newer cars delivered as part of the 1948 order.

The trains departed Wichita at 9:15pm westbound and arrived in Geneseo at 11:45pm; eastbound, No. 412 departed Geneseo at 3:00am and arrived back in Wichita at 6:00am. With minor variations, this was the operating routine of the *Colorado Eagle* for the greater part of its life.

In the late 1940's and early 1950's, the only other through train on the Colorado route was the *Royal Gorge*, Trains 15-16. Like the *Eagles*, these trains connected with the Rio Grande at Pueblo. Instead of traveling north to Denver, however, service to Salt Lake City was routed over Rio Grande's Royal Gorge route through Tennessee Pass. Through Pullman and coach connections for the west coast were made with the Western Pacific at Salt Lake City.

The through Pullman was discontinued with the coming of the *California Zephyr*, however, and by 1950, No. 16 had been downgraded to a Hoisington-Kansas City local. No. 15 then became the St. Louis-Kansas City afternoon train it remained until the arrival of Amtrak in 1971. Coach service beyond Kansas City to Hoisington continued until October, 1954. After that, only the *Colorado Eagles* offered passenger service on the Missouri Pacific route between Kansas City and the Rocky Mountains.

An interesting development that "almost was" was the brush MoPac had with becoming the operator of the St. Louis section of the *California Zephyr*. As early as 1938, officials of the Burlington, Rio Grande, Western Pacific and MoPac gathered in Denver to discuss the feasibility of offering single train service between San Francisco, Chicago and St. Louis.

In complete contrast to what eventually became the *Zephyr's* strongest selling point, however, the initial schedule called for the overnight portions of the run to be the segments through the Rockies and the Sierras, this to accommodate scheduling problems on the Missouri Pacific.

After the first meeting, there was little additional progress on the joint venture for several years. In 1939, the WP, Rio Grande and Burlington announced the inauguration of the *Exposition Flyer*, a through Chicago-San Francisco train that would replace the *Scenic Limited* on the WP. Unlike the streamlined *Zephyr* that eventually replaced it, the *Flyer* was a standard heavyweight coach and sleeper train that lacked commonality of interior decor, dinnerware, menu, or pooled service crew. Still, buoyed by the overwhelming volume of wartime traffic, the train was a success.

Below: Ouch! No information was available regarding the cause of the mishap that left *Colorado Eagle* No. 11 with her nose in the dirt near Pueblo on December 28, 1944. Judging from the small number of onlookers and the absence of the big hook, she hasn't been there long, though. *Charlie Duckworth collection*

By 1943, the stage for a new service was once again set. Representatives from the four railroads met a second time in Denver on August 20. This time, however, reflecting the success of *Burlington's Zephyrs* and MoPac's *Eagles*, no thought was given to operating with standard equipment. Instead, seven complete streamlined consists were ordered: six for daily operations, one to be held in reserve.

A preliminary schedule of 46 hours, 30 minutes was laid out. To maximize the opportunity for marketing western scenery, the schedule called for daylight running through both the Sierras and the Rockies. That decision spelled the end of MoPac participation. Due to off-hours connection times in Denver, it would not be possible to match the existing *Colorado Eagle* schedules. Instead, passengers connecting off the erstwhile "Eagle-Zephyr" in St. Louis would have been faced with a late-night arrival and no opportunity for east coast connections until the following morning.

A last-minute MoPac proposal to move the Denver connection by two hours was rejected by Rio Grande and Western Pacific, and MoPac was left with no choice except to abandon the

Above: Between 1949 and 1952, Missouri Pacific took delivery of 36 Alco PA-1, PA-2 and PA-3 locomotives, including PA-2 8009, shown at St. Louis in 1950. Compared to their EMD brethren, the big beasts had relatively short careers. All were either scrapped or traded-in during the early years of the Jenks administration as MoPac sought to standardize its motive power roster. *Joe Collias photo, Kevin EuDaly collection*

Left: St. Louis-bound No. 12 waits at the joint Rock Island-Rio Grande depot at Colorado Springs in the late 1950's. Northbound, the train used the Santa Fe depot. The third car in the consist is a Rio Grande 24-seat coach-baggage-dormitory car originally built for the Chesapeake & Ohio in 1946. These cars began their D&RGW careers on the overnight Denver-Salt Lake City *Prospector*, and later worked both the *Rio Grande Zephyrs* and the winter Ski Trains. *Charlie Duckworth collection*

project. Thus, a fascinating through-train operation between St. Louis and San Francisco never had the chance to turn a wheel, becoming in the most literal sense a victim of bad timing.

Over the years, the *Colorado Eagles* operated with a wide variety of equipment. Due to the crush of wartime traffic, the original streamlined consists almost immediately had to be expanded with the addition of heavyweight coaches.

Among these were several 6300-series cars that had been extensively rebuilt and repainted into *Eagle* colors at the railroad's Sedalia shops in 1942. Upgrades included tightlock couplers and skirting between the trucks and steps to more nearly match the lightweight cars. The heavyweights were classed as "deluxe" coaches and operated on the *Eagles* and in general service until their retirement in the early 1960's.

Beginning in June, 1942, a third sleeper was added between St. Louis and Denver. This was a heavyweight 8-1-3 car which had been modernized to make them compatible with the new streamlined equipment. Like the Denver-Wichita sleepers, the additional St. Louis car was part of the *Tower* series (*Shrine Tower*, *Beacon Tower*, *Temple Tower*), and operated on an as-required basis to handle overflow traffic or as a stand-in when one of the 6-6-4 Pullmans was being shopped.

After the war, the equipment was reassigned, but returned to the *Colorado Eagle* in 1958 as "Thrift-T-Sleepers." The 8-1-3 cars lasted until 1960, when they were replaced by the tireless 6-6-4's. The newer cars held down the assignment until the "Thrift-T" service was finally discontinued in 1962.

Other "foreign" cars to operate in the consist of the *Eagle* included the 56-seat deluxe coaches and diner-bar-lounges from the original ACF-built *Missouri River Eagle* trainsets. In addition, between 1950 and 1955, a California sleeper was handled between St. Louis and Kansas City. These cars were of the 6-6-4 or 4-4-2 configuration and were relayed to the Rock Island-Espee in Kansas City for the rest of the trip to Los Angeles. This seemingly odd arrangement was necessary because of the poor condition of the Rock Island line between St. Louis and Kansas City. The *Colorado Eagle* was able to run at higher speeds over the St. Louis-Kansas City leg, making it competitive with the Wabash-Union Pacific's *City of St. Louis*, and had an arrival time in Kansas City that neatly coincided with that of the Rock Island train. In 1960, a St. Louis-Kansas City parlor car was added, but this was dropped the following year.

In 1948 and 1949, MoPac purchased 81 new coaches, food service and head-end cars

from old friends ACF and Budd, and another 53 sleepers from Budd and Pullman-Standard. Included in the total were 12 divided, or "Jim Crow" coaches for use in areas of the south and southwest where segregation was practiced.

The sleepers were primarily 10-6 and 14-4 types, although a few oddball 14-1-2 and 5 double bedroom "soda fountain" cars were also included. These last cars were originally planned as observation cars, and are believed to be the only MoPac sleeping cars never to operate on the *Colorado Eagle*.

Although most of the new postwar cars were destined to serve in the southwest on the new *Texas Eagle* and *Valley Eagle*, the order was large enough to more or less re-equip the entire MoPac passenger fleet. Indeed, except for limited forays back into the market in 1952 and 1956, and the purchase of several secondhand

Below: *Colorado Eagle* No. 11 departs St. Louis Union Station on August 29, 1946 with a consist that includes equipment from the 1942 Budd order as well as a coach from the 1940 *Eagle*, a pair of Pullman-Standard 6-6-4 sleepers and a modernized *Tower*-series heavyweight Pullman. And how about those sharp ex-B&O Alton EA's a couple of tracks over? Those babies date from 1937! *Missouri Pacific photo, Charlie Duckworth collection*

C&O coaches and parlor cars acquired in 1950, the 1948-49 deliveries were the last new passenger-carrying cars purchased by the MoPac.

One other sleeper, a 24 single room, 8 double room "Slumbercoach" named *Southland*, was leased from Budd in 1959. Intended for *Texas Eagle* through service between Washington and Texas, it was apparently not judged a success by MoPac, as no other cars of its type were acquired. *Southland* itself was returned to Budd in 1964. It subsequently reappeared as

Northern Pacific's *Loch Tarbert*, and still toils under the same name as Amtrak No. 2090.

The most exciting new equipment in the 1948 order were three Budd-built dome coaches. These cars, called "Planetariums," were designed to match the fluted-side coaches of the original 1942 cars. MoPac touted the "Greater Seeability" from the cars in its May, 1948 timetable: "These sleek-sheathed beauties, to be operated this summer... open up new worlds of scenic grandeur, new thrills in sight-seeing.

They are designed to give you greater travel satisfaction, more convenience, in greater comfort."

The 70-seat Budd domes, numbered 890-892, entered service on June 3, 1948. They were the first of eight eventually owned by the Missouri Pacific, and to many minds, the most attractive. In 1952, the company took delivery on five more Planetarium domes from Pullman-Standard for inclusion in the consists of the San Antonio and Dallas-Fort Worth sections of the

Above and opposite page: A crowd of more than 100,000 was on hand to witness the official opening of Kansas City Union Station on October 30, 1914. Designed by architect Jarvis Hunt of Chicago, the main building enclosed an area of more than 5.5 acres and a waiting room 410 feet long.

The new Union Station replaced an older depot located on Union Street in what became the "West Bottoms" industrial area, and another station known as Grand Central Station that was used by trains of the Chicago Great Western, Kansas City Southern, and Frisco.

On the day it opened, KCUS hosted 207 arrivals and departures operating over 12 railroads. The largest users were the Santa Fe, Burlington, Rock Island and Missouri Pacific, which by itself hosted 43 trains. Other users included UP, KCS, Frisco, Wabash, CGW, Katy, Milwaukee and Alton.

Probably the classiest operations in and out of KCUS were Santa Fe's *Chief* and *Super Chief*, followed by Wabash-UP's *City of St. Louis* and Rock Island's *Golden State*. The station also hosted the country's first streamliners in regular service, including Burlington's original *Zephyr* and UP's M-1000 and *City of Salina*. By the time Amtrak arrived, however, KCUS was down to just 16 trains operating over the MP, UP and ATSF. Burlington Northern had already pulled out of Union Station and was using its own depot in North Kansas City.

The Grand Street bridge just west (left) of the trainsheds was a favorite location for train-watching and photography. In the aerial view taken in the early 1960's, the entire physical plant of the station is visible, including Tower 5 (left) and Tower 6.

Also prominent are the Post Office in the foreground, the "flatiron" Western Auto building, the Liberty Memorial (lower right corner) and, at the top, the muddy Missouri River. The bridge at the right of Union Station is Main Street. *Both photos Arch S. Welch, Kevin EuDaly collection*

Texas Eagles. All the Planetarium cars remained in service on the Texas and Colorado trains, and later on the *Missouri River Eagle* until 1967, when they were sold to the Illinois Central.

A wide variety of meal service was offered. According to an article in the March, 1954 <u>Missouri Pacific Lines Magazine</u>, the *Colorado Eagles* carried a "diner-bar-lounge car" for coach riders and a diner-lounge for Pullman passengers. The coach diner was one of the original *Eagle* cars and was positioned between the first coach and the Planetarium car. The first-class diner ran between the two St. Louis-Denver sleepers.

Entree choices included roast pork, stuffed turkey and Swiss steak. All meals came with potatoes, vegetable, bread, a fruit cup and dessert. Prices ranged between $1.60 and $1.75. Breakfast choices were priced from 50 cents to $1.25. A la carte service (sandwiches or other light meals) was also available at all mealtimes.

The *Colorado Eagles* soldiered on in their full-service configuration through the 1950's and early 1960's, but by then, a cold wind had begun to blow. The Wichita Pullman was discontinued with little protest in February, 1962. The connecting train, which was renumbered 34-35, lasted a little longer, making its final run on the night of January 4, 1965. By that time, hardly anybody noticed.

The real change had come a year earlier, on January 31, 1964, when Pullman and dining car service was discontinued west of Kansas City. East of Kansas City, the train retained most of its amenities, offering for a time Pullman "seat service" on the 6-6-4's, and later a parlor-diner between St. Louis and Kansas City. In March, 1964, the *Colorado Eagle* name disappeared,

Right: Here's another look at *Colorado Eagle* dining car *Cheyenne Mountain*. In this 1963 view, the car has been renumbered 36, rebuilt into a diner-parlor and repainted into the final "Jenks Blue" scheme. Still looks pretty good, doesn't she? *Charlie Duckworth collection*

and for the rest of its life, the train was known by timetable numbers only.

Since the withdrawal of Pullman and dining cars was a service reduction and not an outright discontinuance, there may have been some uncertainty in St. Louis over what would be the public's response. It was far from positive.

Among the first to weigh in was the Missouri Public Service Commission, which formally protested in a letter to the Interstate Commerce Commission. The MPSC complained that, "These trains traverse the state of Missouri, and provide a necessary service for Missouri citizens traveling to and from the states of Kansas and Colorado." The ICC was asked to delay the effective date of the elimination of service pending hearings and a formal decision.

The Kansas Corporation Commission was even less impressed, giving the railroad ten days to restore Pullman and diner service before facing some unspecified penalty (never imposed).

Even local governments got into the act. The town of Lindsborg, Kansas protested to F. J.

Opposite Page: A respectable crowd waits in the rain in August, 1959 for the arrival of westbound No. 11 at Kirkwood, Missouri. Missouri Pacific hospitality is in evidence on this soggy afternoon, as the station agent stands with his umbrella at the ready. *J. Parker Lamb*

Conrad, MoPac's Vice President of Traffic. In a letter dated March 18, 1964, Mr. Carl Hanson of the Lindsborg Chamber of Commerce scolded the railroad not only for de-feathering the *Eagle*, but also for cutting back freight service from daily to every other day.

"Approximately six years ago," Mr. Hanson complained, "this Chamber was working quite closely with Missouri Pacific to interest new industries on this route. It is certainly not conducive to building a business or attracting additional business to have the train service curtailed."

Then, echoing a sentiment repeated at virtually every train-off hearing ever held, he added: "It is our belief that subsidies granted the railroads for many years... entitle our communities to the utmost consideration before action is taken to reduce service."

It was public-be-damned management at its worst, and the public wasn't buying it: "We

are aware of the method of the cutback. First, the Pullman and Diner service; second, probable stop of the Westbound train at Pueblo [as opposed to through-train service] forcing poor connections and layover time to Denver thus eliminating much westbound business; third, a change of time schedule which will eliminate eastbound service in addition to both trains running behind schedule."

Mr. Hanson was more correct than he knew. An internal memo to F. J. Conrad cautioned, in

Below: An E8/E7B/E7 strikes a classic pose at Denver Union Station on the Fourth of July, 1963. At 4:05pm, the EMD trio will power No. 12 on its overnight run to St. Louis. 1963 was the last year the *Colorado Eagle* operated a full consist; beginning in February, 1964, 11-12 became coach-only west of Kansas City. *Louis Marre collection*

part: "Performance of 11-12 has not been satisfactory; 12 missed PRR 30 [at St. Louis] seventeen times last month, and that connection is extremely important for preferential mail. We will probably receive substantial fines, and continued failure to make PRR 30 could jeopardize 11-12's St. Louis-Kansas City RPO Car worth $137,873 per annum."

Interestingly, another significant component of the *Eagle's* express service was newly minted money, which was handled by Rio Grande and MoPac between Denver and the Federal Reserve Bank in Kansas City.

Rio Grande, which at the time was still trying to provide a good service, wasn't much happier. In a series of letters to MoPac Passenger Traffic Manager E. E. Spencer, D&RGW urged its operating partner to consider substituting a grill coach for the now-discontinued diner and possibly restoring at least a summer- season sleeper.

Rio Grande feared losing group travel business and pointed out that the train's 20 minute layover in Pueblo was not sufficient to provide meal service from the depot's lunch counter to passengers hungry after an all-night trip from Kansas City. MoPac demurred, citing the train's graveyard shift hours of operation between Pueblo and Kansas City and the cost of providing a grill coach with an attendant:

"If we furnish a grill-coach on Trains 11-12, manned between Eads-Denver, the expense would simply eat us up. Also, the grill-coach offers limited seating capacity, and would therefore necessitate the handling of an additional full coach during the heavy season. In view of the additional expenses involved, our decision must remain unchanged, insofar as the present arrangements are concerned."

What MoPac did not say publicly was that it was concerned that, by restoring Pullman and food service, patronage might return in sufficient numbers that the outcome of a future ICC discontinuance hearing would be jeopardized.

As it turned out, time was on Missouri Pacific's side. Although the issue of service quality would come up again in connection with Southern Pacific's *Sunset Limited*, the ICC excused itself from further involvement, pleading, as MoPac had correctly anticipated, a lack of jurisdiction. In November, the Kansas Corporation Commission also gave up, but not before reprimanding the railroad for the manner in which the service was trimmed, and ordering "...that the Missouri Pacific make appropriate application to the Commission for the discontinuance of any future services on its passenger trains operating within the state of Kansas."

Rio Grande's plea for reconsideration was equally unpersuasive. Citing annual losses of more than $300,000 from the sleeping and dining cars, Missouri Pacific stuck to its guns, and the services were never restored. Nameless trains 11-12 made their final runs with head-end cars and a single 76-seat coach on April 2, 1966, ending Missouri Pacific passenger service on the lines west of Kansas City.

Sample consist of Train No. 11 at Jefferson City, Missouri, September 19, 1962: IGN E7A 22; MP E7B 18B; MP PA-1 44; MP storage-mail 2404; MP baggage-mail 713; NYC 4-4-2 sleeper *Bear Mountain Bridge*; NYC 4-4-2 sleeper *Imperial Chamber*; D&RGW 6-5-5 sleeper *David Moffatt*; MP 10-6 sleeper *Eagle Haven*; MP diner 840; StLB&M grill coach 824; MP dome-coach 892; MP dormitory-coach 723; MP baggage 702.

Right: One of the classic E's gets a scrubbing at St. Louis in October, 1948. The graceful E7's were the pride of the passenger carrying fleet when this was taken, and she's still got millions of miles left in her. The MoPac bought 14 E7 A-units, three of which were for the IGN, two were for the St. Louis, Brownsville & Mexico, and the rest were MoPac proper. The MoPac also bought 8 B-units. The T&P also bought 10 E7A's, though they didn't go for B-units. The 7017 was the final A-unit for the MoPac, and lasted until scrapping in the late 1960's. *Joe Collias photo, Kevin EuDaly collection*

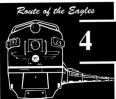

4 Almost an Eagle - *The Sunflower*

Route of the Eagles

The Missouri Pacific Railroad first reached Wichita, Kansas in 1887, following the takeover of the bankrupt St. Louis, Fort Scott & Western Railroad Company. Chartered by a local shippers group in 1881, the StLFS&W managed to lay rails from Fort Scott to Wichita, a distance of 158 miles, before being forced into receivership as a result of a lawsuit over the price of the rails themselves.

Reorganized out of bankruptcy as the Fort Scott, Wichita & Western Railway Company, the little road saw 100% of its reissued stock purchased by Jay Gould and the Missouri Pacific Railway System. The FSW&W was absorbed into another MoPac road, the Kansas & Colorado Pacific in 1891, and subsequently both roads disappeared into the greater Missouri Pacific following a company-wide consolidation in August, 1909.

In February, 1924, Missouri Pacific announced plans to introduce a new luxury train between Wichita and St. Louis. Called the *Sunflower*, the new train made its maiden run on May 4 of that year.

Operating as No. 19 westbound and No. 20 eastbound, the consist included two St. Louis-

Below: The engineer completes his oiling as Missouri Pacific Train 20, the *Sunflower* boards passengers prior to its 7:45pm departure time from Wichita, Kansas. At right is one of the rebuilt heavyweight 8-1-3 sleepers that connected Wichita with the main stem of the *Colorado Eagle* at Geneseo, Kansas. *Lloyd Stagner photo, Charlie Duckworth collection*

43

Above: A decidedly unstreamlined, un-dieselized *Sunflower* connection No. 119 arrives in Omaha behind Mountain 5327 on September 17, 1948. In the consist are 12-1 sleepers from St. Louis, and coaches from Kansas City. The sleepers will return to St. Louis in the consist of Nos. 110-10, the overnight *Missourians*. *Charlie Duckworth collection*

Below: No doubt about where, when or how much it cost! End of the line in Wichita was this Victorian-style depot at the corners of Wichita and Douglas Streets. The station served the *Sunflower* and connecting trains with the *Scenic Limited* and *Colorado Eagle*. The red brick structure fell to the wrecker's ball in 1965. *Missouri Pacific photo, Joe Collias collection*

WICHITA, KANS.

BUILT. 1900   Cost $31,000.00

Wichita 12-1 sleepers, one 12-1 St. Louis-Joplin sleeper, a St. Louis-Wichita dining-lounge, a Durand-Conway Springs (Kansas) cafe-parlor and a Rich Hill-Joplin coach handled in the consist of the Joplin connecting train. Eastbound running time between Wichita and St. Louis was 5:30pm-7:50am for the 484 miles. Westbound, No. 19 departed St. Louis at 7:30pm and arrived in Wichita at 9:55am.

In Wichita, the *Sunflower* used Missouri Pacific's depot located at Wichita and Douglas streets. Completed in 1901 at a cost of $31,000, the three story Victorian brick structure included a 42-foot square waiting room as well as office and storage space.

In addition to the *Sunflower*, the depot also hosted the Wichita-Geneseo section of the *Scenic Limited* (and later, the *Colorado Eagle*) as well as local motor trains between Wichita and small Kansas communities such as Yates Center, Kiowa, Conway Springs, Arkansas City and Hutchinson. The station remained in active service until 1964, when the ticket office and waiting room were closed. In February, 1965, following the discontinuance of *Colorado Eagle* connecting Trains 34-35, the building was finally torn down.

Within a few years of its inauguration, the *Sunflower* had been reorganized into an elaborate maid-of-all-work, forwarding 12-1 Pullman cars between St. Louis and the following cities: Omaha and Lincoln, Nebraska; Joplin,

Missouri; and Wichita and Coffeyville, Kansas. In addition, the Omaha section of the train handled a 12-1 sleeper between Kansas City and Downs, Kansas, and a 16 section car between Kansas City and Omaha. Also in the consist between St. Louis and Wichita were coaches and a diner-lounge.

Complex as they might appear, operations like the *Sunflower* were not unusual. In the 1930's, commercial airline service was unreliable, and not widely available outside of a limited number of subsidized mail routes. Highway travel was little better. Given the uncertain condition of most secondary roads, especially during the winter season, a long-distance auto or bus trip was a chancy proposition at best.

Thus, it fell to the steam railroads and interurbans to provide the only comprehensive national travel network. This they did, with a system of mainline and local trains that picked up and dropped off connecting cars all along their routes. It was another decade before improved highways and automobiles would cause the locals to wither away, leaving simplified mainline operations in their wake.

In the meantime, trains like the *Sunflower* continued to shuffle their consists several times between their eventual end-points. The concept was not unlike the hub-and-spoke systems operated by today's airlines.

To illustrate the *Sunflower's* operations in the mid-1930's, the train departed St. Louis at

4:50pm and arrived in Pleasant Hill at 10:30pm. Reflecting the multiple end-points served, the *Sunflower* operated westbound as timetable numbers 19-119-229-319-419. At Pleasant Hill, the train split into a Kansas City-Omaha section and a Joplin-Wichita section. First to depart at 10:42pm was the Kansas City-Omaha section, now numbered Nos. 19-119. The Joplin-Wichita section, numbered 19-229-319-419, followed at 10:45pm. What had originated in St. Louis as a single train departed Pleasant Hill as two.

First stops for the Wichita section were Harrisonville, then Butler, then Rich Hill, Missouri at 12:19am, where the Wichita and Joplin sections split. In the meantime, Train No. 220-229 had departed Kansas City at 11:45pm for Rich Hill, where it would arrive at 2:45am. At 11:59pm, the *Southerner*, Train No. 115-19 also departed Kansas City for Durand, Kansas, with the St. Louis-Coffeyville Pullman and a Kansas City-Wichita Pullman in tow.

At Rich Hill, No. 220-229 picked up the St. Louis-Joplin sleeper. It then departed as No. 220-229-419 at 2:45am (after no elapsed time in the timetable), and arrived in Joplin at 6:00am. No. 19-319, meanwhile, departed Rich Hill at

12:19am (again, showing no elapsed time). Train 19-319 dropped the Coffeyville Pullman and picked up the Kansas City-Wichita sleeper from No. 115 at Durand.

Following a 3:30am departure, No. 19-319 finally arrived in Wichita at 7:00am. In the consist were the original St. Louis sleepers and the Kansas City Pullman via Durand, plus coaches and the dining car. To round out the operation, No. 313- 319, another local, dropped the St. Louis Pullman in Coffeyville at 7:25am.

On the northern end of the run, the Kansas City section of the *Sunflower* arrived in Kansas City from Pleasant Hill at 11:56pm. It departed three minutes later as No. 119, with St. Louis sleepers bound for Lincoln and Omaha, and a Kansas City Pullman for Downs, Kansas.

The Downs car was set out at Atchison at 1:40am, departing 15 minutes later in the consist of No. 519. Arrival in Downs was at 9:40am. The Omaha sleeper arrived at Union Station in the consist of No. 119 at 7:10am. The Lincoln sleeper arrived in the consist of Union-Lincoln local No. 619 at 7:45am.

Eastbound, the Joplin, Wichita and Coffeyville sections of the *Sunflower* were a mirror image of the westbound operation. The Omaha and Lincoln sleepers, however, were handled in the consist of No. 10, the overnight *Missourian*. In their place, the eastbound *Sunflower's* consist carried a Kansas City-Jefferson City set-out

Above: Class engine PA-1 8001 leads the homely consist of Train 519 at Concordia, Kansas on a cool morning in the early 1950's. No. 519 and companion 520 operated between Downs and Atchison, Kansas, where they connected with Kansas City-Omaha Trains 119-110. *Charlie Duckworth collection*

Below: It takes more than a ticket to get a seat on this car! Not a regular part of the consist of the *Sunflower* or any other MoPac train, but too good to leave out nevertheless. Heavy-weight coach 6166 was built to transport prisoners to and from the state and federal penitentiaries at Leavenworth, Kansas and Jefferson City, Missouri. *Charlie Duckworth collection*

sleeper, and a Denver-St. Louis car that had come east in the consist of nameless No. 14 between Denver and Kansas City.

By the mid-1940's, declining patronage and wartime restrictions on short-haul sleeping car routes had significantly altered the *Sunflower's* operations. Gone from the timetable were the through Pullmans formerly operated between St. Louis and Joplin, Coffeyville, Lincoln, and Downs.

Passengers bound for these points now traveled in the mainline train as far as Pleasant Hill or Kansas City. From there, they completed their journeys in coaches handled in the consists of various local connecting trains. As in previous years, through Pullman service was still available between St. Louis, Wichita and Omaha.

New in the consist of No. 119 were a Kansas City-Downs through coach and a Kansas City-Omaha dining car that must have done a brisk breakfast business, considering the train's pokey seven-and-a-half hour carding over the 199 mile route. Eastbound, the 1943 *Sunflower* handled a Wichita-St. Louis dining car, Wichita-St. Louis coaches, a Kansas City-St. Louis coach and a Los Angeles-St. Louis 6-6-4 Pullman that traveled between the west coast and Kansas City in the consist of Southern Pacific- Rock Island No. 4, the *Golden State*.

With only minor changes, this was the *Sunflower's* basic operating scheme until its eventual discontinuance. In 1948, the dining car was replaced by a grill coach, and the 12-1 Pullman was replaced by one of the new 14-4 cars ordered from Pullman-Standard in 1945.

In 1950, departure from St. Louis was changed from 5:40 to 5:00pm. This had the effect of slowing the train's running time by 40 minutes, since arrival in Wichita was not similarly advanced.

Also in 1950, the 14-4 sleeper was changed again, this time to a "Cascade" series 10-5 sleeper. Although painted in regular *Eagle* blue and gray, the 10-5's were not Missouri Pacific cars, but belonged to the Baltimore and Ohio.

Prior to being released to the *Sunflower*, they had operated between Washington, D.C. and Fort Worth, Texas as part of the *Texas Eagle's* through Pullman service. In 1952, the *Sunflower* was finally dieselized. However, except for the 14-4, and later 10-5 sleepers, the trains were never regularly assigned streamlined cars.

Whatever ideas Missouri Pacific might have had about its Wichita and Omaha operations, by the early 1950's the company had clearly determined that five mainline trains on St. Louis-Kansas City runs were too many. Accordingly, the main stem of the *Sunflower* was discontinued in May, 1954.

The demise of the mainline train did not spell the end of the *Sunflower's* service, how-ever, as various portions of the operation survived in other trains. If one were to take the railroad's public position at face value, the *Sunflower* was not so much discontinued as it was "absorbed" into other operations. Indeed, the St. Louis-Kansas City part of the schedule so nearly matched that of the more luxurious *Colorado Eagle* that it is doubtful if Nos. 19-20 were missed at all.

With respect to the Wichita Pullman, the railroad reasoned that one overnight train was pretty much like another one, especially after the lights were out. Accordingly, after the Pleasant Hill connection was broken, the Wichita-St. Louis sleeper operated in the consist of Trains 9-10, the Kansas City-St. Louis *Missourians*. West of Kansas City, the sleeper was forwarded by Trains 125-126 to Durand, Kansas, and then by Durand-Wichita locals 425-426 over the remainder of the run.

This combination lasted until February, 1956. At that time, the locals were dropped, and with them, the last through train service of any

Below: Another look at Atchison-Downs connection at Concordia, this time in the charge of 1,000 horsepower EMD AA6 built for the *Delta Eagle*, 7100. With its relatively light axle loadings, the single-engined unit was especially well suited to working branchline operations like Nos. 519-520. *Charlie Duckworth collection*

kind between St. Louis and Wichita. After that, the only rail route between the two cities was via a connection with the Santa Fe at Kansas City.

Another surviving *Sunflower* service was Trains 119-110, the Kansas City-Omaha connection. Whether the railroad was sensitive to appearances is not known, but following the discontinuance of the mainline train, the Omaha service was listed in the December, 1954 timetable as trains 11-119 and 110-10. This made the

westbound run nominally the Kansas City-Omaha section of the *Colorado Eagle*, even though no direct service was available to or from either end point.

This masquerade lasted only until the April, 1955 timetable, when 119-110 were more correctly carded as stand-alone operations. The trains were finally dropped on October 8, 1959. With that final cutback, the ghost of the *Sunflower* was laid to rest once and for all.

Above: After the demise of the *Sunflower*, MoPac continued to offer passenger service between St. Louis and Wichita by way of a connection at Pleasant Hill, Missouri. In the summer of 1955, minimalist Train 425 seems to be doing a fair express business at El Dorado, Kansas. Following this station stop, 425 will be in Wichita in less than an hour.
Chris Brickley photo, Lee Berglund collection

Right: End of the line. Steam generator-equipped F3 564 powers Atchison-Downs Train 519 through Downs on a chilly morning in April, 1959. The little *Sunflower* remnant is enjoying her last full year of operation; she'll tie up for the last time on November 15, 1960. *W. Gibson, Sr. photo, Lee Berglund collection*

Above: Missouri Pacific President L. W. Baldwin would surely be delighted with Mountain 5325's clear stack as she scorches the ballast on her way to Kansas City with the *Kay-See Flyer* **in the 1940's. The well-kept right-of-way, lush foliage and blue water of the Missouri River make this a postcard-perfect vignette of MoPac steam-era railroading.** *Steve Beleck collection*

Right: Regular gas is selling for 23 cents a gallon as a PA-3 powered Gulf Coast Lines passenger run drifts through Beaumont, Texas in March, 1956. During the period, GCL operated two pairs of passenger trains on the line between Houston and New Orleans, the daylight *Orleaneans* **and the overnight** *Houstonians*. *Kevin EuDaly collection*

Opposite page top: T&P's *Texas Eagle* is still in the glory days with two E-units spliced by a T&P F7B. The lead E7 was the last of two of the glamour girls purchased by the T&P in April, 1949, which brought their total to ten. A clear January day in 1962 finds the gorgeous *Eagle* at Big Spring, Texas. *Paul Meyer*

Opposite page bottom: D&RGW F7 5654 and T&P E8 33 await departure time on the point of MoPac Train 12, the former *Colorado Eagle* at Denver Union Station on August 26, 1964. Looks like the last car in the train - likely a coach by this late date - has also been furnished by the Rio Grande. *Charles Zeiler*

Below: Passenger Geep 322 gets ready to move Little Rock-bound Train 32 out of Alexandria, Louisiana on a hot August 14, 1966. The remnant of the once-prestigious *Sunshine Special* handled a Little Rock coach and a 14-4 sleeper to St. Louis. That first baggage car must have passed through a Texas dust storm since its last trip to the washer! *Barry Carlson*

Above: Mention the name *Aztec Eagle* and images arise of a full-service luxury flyer between the midwest and sunny Mexico. Well, here she is: MoPac No. 1, the *Aztec Eagle*, with a coach and a 10-6 St. Louis sleeper, plodding through south Texas bound for Laredo in the summer of 1966. The coach was known locally as the "merchandise car" due to the habit of Mexican customs agents not noticing the contents of the car on its return trips from the U.S. *Bruce Petty*

Opposite page top: Toward the end of the passenger service, MoPac's E7's were finally retired, leaving what remained of the *Eagle* in the care of the road's newer E8's and boiler-equipped GP7's. On October 21, 1968, E8 40 leads the *Texas Eagle* on the outskirts of Austin, Texas. *John Gwinn photo, Dan Pope collection*

Opposite page bottom: Roscoe, Texas, junction point between the T&P and the Roscoe, Snyder and Pacific, does not rate so much as flag stop status for the *Texas Eagles*, nor, for that matter, for secondary Trains 27- 28. Nevertheless, *Eagle* No. 21 prepares to snag a pouch of mail as it pounds through town on January 2, 1964. *Joe McMillan*

Left: E8 35 powers the short consist of *Texas Eagle* No. 2 into Austin, Texas on October 25, 1969. Incredibly, the fare between Austin and St. Louis still includes a $1.50 reserved seat charge. With a consist of a single diner-lounge and a couple of coaches, it's hard to believe there's still a need for assigned seats. *Steve Patterson*

Above: Photographer Paul Meyer recalls making numerous trips to photograph trains during his college years, including visits to the Frisco, Santa Fe and Missouri Pacific in southeastern Kansas. Here, during one of his outings, he captured *Rainbow Special* 126, southbound at Paola, in the summer of 1955. *Paul Meyer*

Opposite page top: An Alco PA and a pair of E7's back the *Texas Eagle* into the massive trainshed at St. Louis Union Station on a clear winter morning. Today, the scene looks quite different, as Union Station has been turned into a hotel and shopping center, and a freeway overpass runs through the foreground. *Walter Petras photo, Richard Wallin collection*

Opposite page bottom: A perfectly matched train is ready to roll at Houston, Texas behind E8A 41. Little blue and gray remains at this late date in April, 1968, this train bearing out the fact that the end is only a scant three years away. Soon enough, the train itself will pass into the pages of history, gone but not forgotten. *Ralph Back*

Above: E8 24 and a passenger geep does the honors on Train 21, the New Orleans-Fort Worth section of the *Texas Eagle*. By this late date, El Paso service had been discontinued, and Nos. 21-22 operated New Orleans-Fort Worth only. *K. B. King, Jr. photo, Dan Pope collection*

Right: B-o-o-a-a-r-r-d! The conductor of *Texas Eagle* No. 22 enjoys the sunshine in Fort Worth, Texas prior to the train's 3:50pm departure time on May 11, 1969. With his crisp white shirt, spotless blue uniform and those T&P emblems in his lapels, he still embodies the pride the railroad once took in its premier operation. *Steve Patterson*

Opposite page top: Faded paint and a scarred, grime-streaked pilot provide eloquent testimony to the countless miles rolled up by E7 4. Originally acquired in 1947 as T&P 2003, the weary warrior is now in the twenty-first (and final) year of her MoPac career on this July afternoon in 1968. *Mac Owen photo, Kevin EuDaly collection*

Opposite page bottom: Trains 37-38 ran between Hot Springs and Memphis, and handled a 10-6 sleeper to Chicago and a 14-4 car to St. Louis. In this December 27, 1962 scene, GP7 328 gets ready to move a five-car No. 38 out of the Hot Springs depot for Little Rock an hour and 20 minutes down the line. *Louis Marre*

Opposite page top: An E7/E8 combination lead Train 22 out of Dallas Union Station on February 20, 1968. By the time the *Texas Eagle* was finally discontinued in May, 1969, it was the last passenger train to serve the Dallas-Fort Worth market. Today, Amtrak's *Texas Eagle*, operating over the former rails of the Missouri Pacific once again calls at Dallas Union Station. *Steve Patterson*

Opposite page bottom: In 1964, Texas and Pacific ran day trains 23-24 between New Orleans and Marshall, Texas, where they connected with mainline trains of the MoPac for points in south and west Texas. On December 30, 1964, the former *Louisiana Daylight* pays a call at the massive depot in Marshall. *Louis Marre*

Right: Passenger GP7's 336 and 327 power the westbound six-car *Texas Eagle* at Fort Worth in 1967. Included in the consist this day are I-GN mail-baggage 378, MP baggage-dormitory 365, Budd 10-6 sleeper *Eagle View*, MP diner-coach 582 and coaches 403 and 450. Following the end of passenger service in 1971, diner 582 was converted to air brake instruction car 20. *K. B. King, Jr. photo, Dan Pope collection*

Below: Here's an "in-your-face" look at Alco PA-2 8015 laying over at Pacific, Missouri in June, 1960, with the three-car consist of Train 35-36, known informally as the "Pacific Eagle." Faced with increased competition and rising costs, Nos. 35-36 made their last runs on December 15, 1961. *Richard Wallin*

Above: The *Texas Eagle* toward the end of its days was generally powered by E8's and boiler equipped geeps. Here E8A 41 has a five-car consist rolling near Austin, Texas on September 16, 1968. *John Gwinn photo, Dan Pope collection*

Opposite page top: A perfectly matched A-B-A set of E-units lead a perfectly matched set of equipment on the *Texas Eagle* at St. Louis in late 1959. MoPac streamliners didn't get much prettier than this. *Richard Wallin*

Opposite page bottom: Here's a pretty-as-you-please view of Train 14, eastbound at Pleasant Hill on September 24, 1967. The company obviously isn't turning much profit on the revenue generated by this three-car job, and yet the pride of the road is evident in the glossy paint and the more-than-ample power available to get her over the road. *Steve Patterson*

Opposite page top: An eight-car *Texas Eagle* arrives at St. Louis on a balmy morning in April, 1964. That chocolate-and-orange car in the background is lettered for Illinois Central's every-other-day Chicago-St. Louis-Florida *City of Miami*. *Dan Pope collection*

Opposite page bottom: Texas & Pacific E8 33 heads an E7B and 11 cars on St. Louis-bound train 16 at Kansas City Union Station on May 2, 1965. In the background, a Katy E8 dressed in Deramus red awaits her next assignment on the point of the *Katy Flyer*, or possibly the *Texas Special*. *Robert Malinoski*

Left: PA-3 8033 powers Omaha-Kansas City Train 110 at Union, Nebraska on an overcast May 30, 1959. At Kansas City, passengers from No. 110 will be able to connect with Train 10, the *Missourian*, for the overnight run to St. Louis. *Dan Pope collection*

Below: Looks like there's plenty of power to move the *Texas Eagle* out of St. Louis on this August evening in 1966. After the west and south Texas sections of the *Eagle* were combined in 1961, the unified train often ran 20 or more cars long between St. Louis and Little Rock. *J. W. Swanberg*

Above: With a trailing consist of L&N blue and gray equipment, an F-unit trio prepares to depart Dearborn Station with the combined *Hummingbird-Georgian* in October, 1967. Before the year was out, the train had been discontinued, leaving Trains 3-4 as the last vestiges of C&EI varnish. *Dan Pope collection*

Below: Freshly repainted C&EI E7 27 soaks up the sun at Houston Union Station on October 7, 1967. The unit was originally purchased by the C&EI in 1946 as no. 1100, and powered streamliners such as the *Whippoorwill* and *Meadowlark* between Chicago and southern Illinois. *Randy Drolen collection*

Rail passenger service between St. Louis and the East first became available in 1857, when the Ohio & Mississippi (later the Baltimore & Ohio) reached the east bank of the Mississippi River at Illinoistown (now East St. Louis).

It was almost another two decades, however, before taking the train to St. Louis actually meant arriving in St. Louis by rail. Prior to that time, passengers traveling via the St. Louis, Vandalia and Terre Haute (later the Pennsylvania), Ohio & Mississippi, and others were obliged to disembark in East St. Louis and cross the Mississippi River by ferry.

Trains from the west, including those of the Pacific Railroad (Missouri Pacific), North Missouri (Wabash), and Iron Mountain had no need to cross the river, and so built their own depots in or near the downtown area. With the opening of the Eads Bridge and the double-track tunnel

between the Bridge and the Mill Creek Valley rail yards on July 4, 1874, trains from the east could now enter the city directly.

This did not happen right away. Even though the bridge was available for use, the railroads from the east claimed that their Illinois charters did not give them the right to operate in the state of Missouri, and the bridge company had no authority to operate trains anywhere.

The problem was partially resolved the following year, when terminal companies were formed to handle freight traffic, but passenger trains still terminated across the river. Eventually, on June 13, 1875, the first passenger train crossed the Eads Bridge and dropped its passengers at the new Union Depot.

The St. Louis Union Depot Company was formed on May 9, 1874 to erect a depot on Poplar Street, between Ninth and Twelfth. The Company acted under authority granted by the Missouri legislature in 1871 to erect union depots

and stations throughout the state. The Poplar Street site was chosen at the end of a two-year study.

In terms of travel convenience, the new Depot was a great step forward in that trains from all railroads serving the city were able to arrive and depart from a central location. The new station included waiting rooms, ticket offices and 11 covered arrival and departure tracks.

Below: St. Louis Union Station is viewed looking eastward along Market Street. In the foreground is "The Meeting of the Waters," symbolizing St. Louis' position at the confluence of the Missouri, Mississippi and Meramec Rivers. The station thrives today as a combined hotel-theater-shopping complex. *Irv Schankman photo, courtesy Dorrill Photo Services*

Above: The "nerve center" of St. Louis Union Station was Perry Tower, built in the summer of 1940 following a fire that destroyed the original tower. Perry Tower controlled access to the 42 tracks leading into the station. Day operations at the Tower required the services of 11 people, including a Passenger Train Master, a Chief Train Director, two Assistant Train Directors, an Operator, a Teleautograph Operator, a Power Director and four Levermen. *TRRA Historical and Technical Society collection*

Right: The predominance of military uniforms betray the wartime origin of this July 24, 1942 photo, taken from the stairway leading from the Great Hall downstairs to the ticket office. The mural above the counter depicts the meeting of the railroads with the once-important riverboat trade on the St. Louis levee. In the mural's background is Eads Bridge, the first bridge to carry railroad traffic across the Mississippi River. *TRRA Historical and Technical Society collection*

At the time it opened, the new Union Depot served 14 trains per day.

By 1893, its last full year of operation, that number had increased to 124. Such growth quickly rendered the Union Depot obsolete, and by 1890, plans were underway for a larger structure. A national architectural competition with a ten thousand dollar first prize was announced in March, 1891. The winning design was submitted by the firm of Link and Cameron, of St. Louis. Principal partner Theodore C. Link was placed in charge of the project.

Located on Market Street between Eighteenth and Twentieth Streets, the new St. Louis Union Station opened on September 1, 1894. The Market Street location was selected by the first president of the Terminal Railroad Association, William A. Taussig, because it was the closest area to downtown that could accommodate a structure the size of the winning design. As was the case until 1980, the station was owned and operated by the TRRA.

As the railroad gateway to St. Louis, the new station was designed along the lines of the French walled city of Carcassone, itself a gateway during the Middle Ages. The Romanesque head building was 606 feet long, 80 feet deep, and featured a 230-foot tall clock tower with a four-faced clock, whose dials were ten feet in diameter.

Above: On December 19, 1958, holiday travelers crowd the Midway as they wait to board multiple sections of Missouri Pacific's *Texas Eagle*. In 1942, a glass and steel wall replaced the previous wrought iron gates separating the Midway from the train shed. The gates yielded 75 tons of scrap metal for the War Drive. *Wayne Leeman photo, TRRA Historical and Technical Society collection*

Below: Clerks load westbound mail aboard MP No. 9, the *Missourian* on the night of April 22, 1958. The mail gondolas had come underground from the main post office across 18th Street from Union Station. Pneumatic lifts served most of the tracks under the train shed, raising the mail from the tunnel to the platform level. *Wayne Leeman photo, TRRA Historical and Technical Society collection*

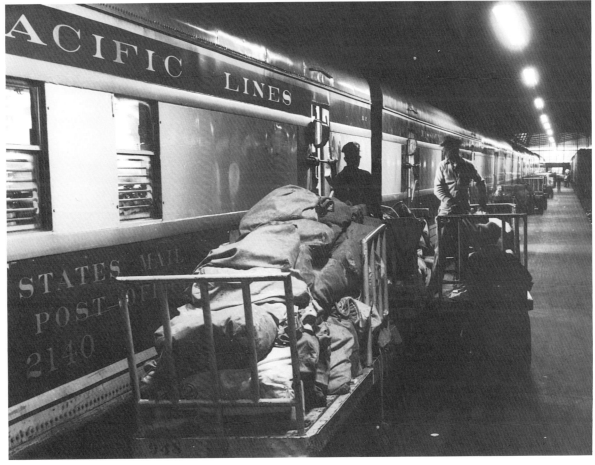

Outside walls facing the street were built of Indiana limestone, with the rear wall built from gray and buff brick. The central pavilion featured twin turrets and a porte-cochere that was removed in 1911 when Market Street was widened. The roof was covered with gray tiles that were replaced with the present red tiles in 1949.

Within the station's walls was a 100-room hotel, an 8,500 square foot Grand Hall with a 65-foot barrel-vaulted ceiling, and a two-story, 30 x 300 foot baggage room. A 4,500 pound iron chandelier that held 350 lights helped illuminate the Grand Hall. The chandelier lasted until World War II, when it was sacrificed for scrap.

Between the headhouse and trainshed was a 70-foot wide "Midway," which was the principal waiting area for those meeting arriving trains or bidding farewell to departing travelers. At its center was a huge message board containing scheduled arrival and departure times for all trains, as well as information regarding expected delays. The Midway was open to the street at both ends, and included a Fred Harvey restaurant, lockers, and a newsstand.

The train shed was an architectural marvel in its own right, spanning 606 feet in width and 630 feet in length. It covered an area of nearly nine acres under roof with 32 arrival and departure tracks. An ornamental wrought iron fence separated the train shed from the Midway. This was also sacrificed to the wartime scrap drive, and was replaced by a glass and steel "air wall" that had 16 doorways providing entry to the platforms.

Altogether, the head building, Midway, and train shed enclosed more than 11 acres under roof. Within the station system were 19 miles of

Below: Another view of Union Station, looking west along Market Street in the winter of 1966. The clock tower stood 230 feet tall, with clock faces 10 feet in diameter. The headhouse building was two blocks long, spanning the 600-plus feet between 18th and 20th Streets. *Larry Thomas*

track, including 3-1/2 miles beneath the train shed. The entire project cost more than $6.5 million, a fabulous sum at the time.

Because railroad access to the Market Street site was limited to a narrow valley, there was no opportunity to construct a through station that would require a large number of east-west tracks and platforms. For this reason, it was decided that the new Union Station would have to be built as a stub terminal. This meant that no trains passed through the station without reversing directions.

Standard practice was for trains to enter the yards at the south end of the station and pull past the trainshed before backing through a series of complicated double-throat approach tracks and into the station. Only Missouri Pacific commuter trains operated in later years pulled directly into the station, this to save time for anxious commuters.

Improvements to the station commenced within a few years of opening, including lengthening of the trainshed by 180 feet, and the construction of a new signal tower in 1902. In anticipation of increased traffic from the 1904 World's Fair, a tunnel was built so that baggage and mail handling operations could be moved underground.

A special car storage yard, known as "Pastime Yard" was also built near Page Avenue. This was removed following the closing of the Fair. In 1929, ten additional tracks were built on the west side of the station, bringing the total to 42. These tracks were not installed under the original train shed, however. Instead, new platforms with umbrella sheds were constructed.

The expansion solidified Union Station's claim on having the greatest number of tracks on one level of any station in the world. Also in 1929, the Midway was finally heated, eliminating a source of complaints from virtually everyone who passed through the city during the winter months.

At its peak, Union Station saw the arrival and departure of 269 daily trains operated by 22 railroads, including a number of "accommodation" (commuter) trains running over the Frisco and Missouri Pacific. By 1933, however, commuter services had dwindled considerably, as Frisco exited the business and Missouri Pacific was down to six round trips per day.

In July, 1940, a fire destroyed the signal tower, causing the suspension of all remaining MoPac commuter trains except for a single St. Louis-Pacific train that hung on until 1961. "Engineer" on the first train to back into the train shed following completion of the new tower in November, 1940, was author-rail historian Lucius Beebe.

After 1920, intercity rail passenger traffic through St. Louis began a long decline that was interrupted only briefly during World War II. As an example of the crush of traffic created by the War, in 1943, 1,347,998 tickets were sold, and the Fred Harvey restaurant served 2,714,570 meals, or nearly 8,000 per day. Also in that year, 72,621 trains, 660,000 cars and 22 million people passed through the terminal complex. It was truly a sight to behold, but unfortunately, it didn't last.

By 1950, the number of daily trains handled had dropped to 147, and by 1957 to only 115. In 1971, immediately prior to the arrival of Amtrak, passenger service in and out of St. Louis was down to 11 train pairs: three each over the Missouri Pacific and Gulf, Mobile & Ohio, two over the Penn Central and one pair each over the Norfolk & Western, Louisville & Nashville and B&O.

After Amtrak Conveyance Day, this was cut further to two pairs of trains over the GM&O and a single New York-Kansas City train operated jointly by the Penn Central and Missouri Pacific.

By the late 1970's, low utilization combined with high maintenance costs and the increasing deterioration of the building forced Amtrak to seek other quarters. The search ended with the construction of a prefabricated "Amshack" depot a few blocks east, at 550 South Sixteenth Street. Plans for a more permanent, intermodal facility have yet to get off the drawing board, and at this writing, the "temporary" station has now passed its sixteenth birthday.

The last Amtrak passenger train to operate from St. Louis Union Station was the Chicago-bound *Ann Rutledge*. The date was October 31, 1978. The final departure was accorded considerable coverage by the local media and railfans, including a musical send-off by a New Orleans-style jazz band that stood on the platform and played funeral marches throughout the boarding.

Plans for alternative use for the station had been proposed as early as 1945. These included a combined rail-bus-air terminal, a heliport, a concert hall, a natural history museum, a theatre, and a shopping mall. For various reasons, none of these schemes ever came to fruition. Finally, in 1980, the station was acquired by Oppenheimer Properties, of New York. Aided by a grant from the Department of Housing and Urban Development, a $135 million redevelopment project was begun in 1983.

In August, 1985, the station was reopened as a combined hotel-specialty retail-entertainment complex. The station's Grand Hall was meticulously restored to its original condition, including the famous "Whispering Arch" over the front doors. The design of this arch is such that a person standing at one end can whisper to a person standing at the other end and be clearly heard.

In its refurbished condition, the Grand Hall now serves as the lobby for the 550-room hotel. The former Midway and train shed enclose 160,000 square feet of retail space, a one-acre lake where visitors can rent small paddleboats, and a covered parking area for 2,000 vehicles. For once, the story has a happy ending: From the day it opened, the new St. Louis Union Station has been a runaway success, attracting crowds not seen since the heyday years during World War II.

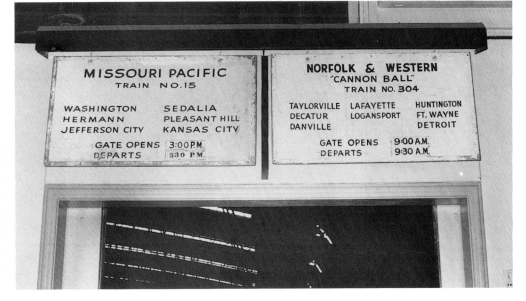

Right: Metal train signs were hung above the doorways between the Midway and the train shed to announce departure times for trains leaving St. Louis Union Station. On this summer day in 1968, Missouri Pacific's nameless No. 15 and N&W's *Cannon Ball* shared a platform on the west side of the station. *Larry Thomas*

White River: Route of the *Southern Scenic*

Although primarily regarded as a St. Louis-based carrier, the Missouri Pacific Railroad did operate three pairs of passenger trains between Kansas City, Little Rock and Memphis, over two separate lines. Of the two routes, the least known, and unquestionably the more scenic, was the White River Line.

Built as a shortcut for freight between the southeast and Kansas City, the White River Railway was completed in December, 1905, between Carthage, Missouri, on the MP, and Diaz, Arkansas on the Iron Mountain.

The White River Line was eventually absorbed through a series of reorganizations into the parent company, thereby losing its identity as an individual carrier. It remained a part of the MoPac until 1993, when the route from Pleasant Hill to Diaz Junction was spun off to short line operator Missouri & Northern Arkansas.

The White River was constructed through some of the most spectacular but sparsely popu-lated territory on the entire railroad. System maps in public timetables published well into the 1960's highlighted the area between Bates-ville, Arkansas and Branson, Missouri as "White River Country."

Largely inaccessible except by rail (or per-haps water), the 161-mile segment through the Ozark Mountains boasted towering limestone palisades, five tunnels of between 660 and 3,455 feet, and 52 water crossings on bridges ranging up to 913 feet long and 122 feet high.

As originally built, there were 57 wooden trestles in the 96 miles between Cotter, Arkansas and Crane, Missouri alone. By 1925, however, all but ten had been replaced by earth fills, as the railroad had determined that fills were more permanent and no more expensive than rebuild-ing the bridges. By the time it was completed, the trestle replacement project had consumed 3.4 million cubic yards of earth and 12,000 yards of concrete drainage culverts reinforced by 500 tons of steel bar.

Passenger service over the White River line began on June 7, 1931, with the inaugura-tion of the new *Southern Scenic*. So named because it was intended as a southeastern con-nection with MoPac's main line flyer, the *Scenic Limited*, the train was given a grand send-off at Memphis Union Station prior to its maiden run. A bottle of Mountain Valley water from Hot Springs was broken across the locomotive pilot by Miss Memphis, Lena Thomas, who chris-tened the train in the presence of newspapermen, Chamber of Commerce, and Missouri Pacific officials. Connections with the *Scenic Limited* were at Geneseo, Kansas, by way of Wichita.

MoPac's Assistant Vice President-Passen-ger Traffic, Paul J. Neff, remarked that the new train had been instituted in recognition of Mem-

Below: *Southern Scenic* No. 221 loads ex-press packages during a station stop at Bergman, Arkansas in 1958. StLB&M GP7 4253 was one of a group of 52 units equipped with steam generators for passenger service. *Wayne Leeman photo, Kevin EuDaly collection*

Missouri Pacific

— The Southern Scenic
— The Southerner and Rainbow Special

mak map - 1995

City *Southern Scenic*, Trains 219-232-215 and 212-231-224. The actual through trains were Nos. 219-224; the other numbers reflected the Kansas City-Pleasant Hill portion of the schedule, and a Joplin connection that joined the mainline operation at Carthage, Missouri.

Routing for the 538-mile run was Kansas City-Pleasant Hill over the Sedalia Subdivision, then south on the Carthage Sub to Carthage, Missouri. From there, the line turned southeast through Aurora and Branson to Diaz, Arkansas on the old Iron Mountain main line. At Bald Knob, the train left the main for the final 91-mile leg into Memphis. Through service to Wichita was no longer being promoted.

In 1941, the *Southern Scenic* offered heavyweight baggage-coach and coach-parlor-diner service in both directions. Departure from Kansas City was at 7:50am with arrival in Memphis at 10:30pm. On the return trip, No. 224 departed Memphis at 7:45am and arrived in Kansas City at 9:25pm.

Conditional and positive stops included just about every kink in the tracks, with principal stops at Bald Knob, Newport and Batesville, Arkansas, and at Hollister, Branson, Carthage and Pleasant Hill, Missouri. The Joplin section departed at 10:40am and connected at Carthage

phis' growing importance as a gateway city, and that it was the first step in a "definitely planned program to provide complete and adequate service between all Missouri Pacific points." Mr. Neff went on to say that the new service "provides an ideal route for the vacation or business traveler, as well as a direct line for expedited freight movement."

Riders aboard the inaugural trip included leaders of the chambers of commerce from Memphis, Kansas City, Wichita and Little Rock, as well as members of the press from each of those cities. Upon arrival in Wichita the following morning, the train received a second christening by Miss Evelyn Watkins, daughter of the president of the Wichita Chamber of Commerce. Departure from Memphis was at 8:00am, with arrival in Kansas City at 9:45pm. Connections from Little Rock were made with Train 4 at Bald Knob at 9:45am.

Despite the initial outpouring of optimism, however, and the seemingly surefire opportunity to market the White River Line as a scenic

attraction, few passengers ever actually got to see it.

According to the February, 1933 public timetable, the only MoPac passenger service over the route was still the Memphis-Kansas

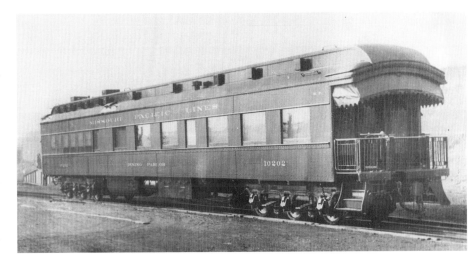

Above: Here's a close look at diner-parlor 10202. This car and sister 10201 were out-shopped by ACF in 1929. They seated 13 in the parlor section and 18 in the dinette-not a bad first-class service for what amounted to a branch line operation. *Charlie Duckworth collection*

Left: How about those snazzy summer straws! It's just past three o'clock in the afternoon as Train 232, the Memphis-bound *Southern Scenic* catches her breath at the Branson, Missouri depot in the summer of 1944. That brass railed obs on the rear is likely parlor-diner 10201 or 10202. *Charlie Duckworth collection*

Right: Rakish E6 7003 powers Kansas City-bound No. 126 at Fort Smith, Arkansas on a sultry August evening in 1958. That Frisco RPO at right will shortly be heading north in the consist of SLSF Train 704, the Paris, Oklahoma-Monett, Missouri connection with the crack *Meteor*. *Louis Marre*

Below: Southbound *Rainbow* No. 125 conducts business at Fort Smith, Arkansas on a pleasant evening in June, 1957. Following a 6:20pm departure, the *Rainbow* is scheduled for an even dozen positive and conditional stops during the rest of the 124-mile run into Little Rock. *Louis Marre*

Below: MoPac 4-6-2 6444 provides the power for the *Southern Scenic*, running southbound at Branson, Missouri on September 10, 1947. The classy little train sits at the bottom of opposing 1.0 percent grades; she'll be barking on the way out of town. *Joe Collias collection*

Above: Business is brisk for the *Rainbow*, shown here at Wagoner, Oklahoma in June, 1958, as the consist includes a heavyweight combination-coach and two rebuilt heavyweight coaches. Switch rods in the foreground and that '50 Mercury complete with "suicide doors" parked at the left just behind E7 7008 makes the scene complete. *Jerry Moore photo, Louis Marre collection*

Below: Freshly-painted E7 7012 is on the point of an all-heavyweight consist as *Rainbow* 126 loads passengers at Van Buren, Arkansas on December 30, 1956. The train is coach-only, having lost its grill-coach in April of that year. *Louis Marre*

at 11:05am. Arrival back in Joplin was at 6:25pm, following a 5:35pm Carthage connection.

In November, 1949, the *Scenic's* timetable numbers were changed to 210-221-222 southbound and 231-232-211 northbound. At the same time, the schedule was reversed, making the train an overnighter. New running times between Kansas City and Memphis were 11:50pm-5:00pm southbound and 12:30am-6:15pm northbound (so much for scenery!).

Consistent with the train's revised schedule, the diner was exchanged for a grill coach, and a heavyweight 10-1-2 Pullman was added to the consist. This arrangement lasted only a brief time before the sleeper was withdrawn in 1952.

In 1953, the through portion of the run was cut back from Memphis to Newport, Arkansas.

This was the southern end point for the rest of the *Scenic's* career. Arrival at Newport was at 1:25pm, which permitted timely connections only with No. 3, the St. Louis-Little Rock *Ozarker*.

This effectively ended direct Kansas City-Memphis service over the MoPac, leaving such market as there was to Frisco's *Sunnyland* and *Kansas City-Florida Special*. A year later, the grill coach was dropped, leaving the train coach-only. Time was running out for the *Southern Scenic*.

In 1957, the service was cut back again. Although MoPac doubtless saved terminal costs in Kansas City, the move resulted in a nowhere-to-nowhere Newport-Pleasant Hill run. Timetable numbers were changed to 221-232. At the same time, the *Scenic* lost its name, providing further indication, if any was needed, of the estate to which it had declined in the estimation of MoPac management.

In April, 1959, the railroad filed a discontinuance petition with the ICC. In an accompanying press release, MoPac President Russell Dearmont claimed the trains were losing more than $175,000 per year on an out-of-pocket basis.

At the hearings, protesters pointed out, among other things, that eliminating the trains would leave a number of communities without rail service, a hardship in adverse weather given the mountainous terrain traversed by the line. Carthage Mayor Robert Eddy claimed that dropping the service would result in an annual payroll loss to the city of more than $100,000.

Witnesses also unified in their belief that the trains would do a better business if they ran all the way through to Kansas City, instead of terminating in Pleasant Hill. Despite these ob-

jections, however, the ICC ruled in MoPac's favor and the trains made their final runs on March 22, 1960.

Southeast via Southwest: The *Southerner* and the *Rainbow Special*

Though lacking the scenic interest of the White River Line, MoPac's other southeastern route operated in an area of somewhat greater population density, and consequently higher revenue potential. Despite this apparent advantage, however, the Kansas City-Little Rock trains turned out to be no more successful, disappearing from the timetable literally within days of their White River counterparts.

Except at Kansas City Union Station, MoPac trains bound for Little Rock shared no trackage with trains operating over the White River line. Instead, they began their southeasterly journey by heading southwest from Kansas City through Osawatomie and Durand to Coffeyville, Kansas.

At Okay, Oklahoma, junction point for the MoPac and subsidiary Kansas, Oklahoma and Gulf, the line turned southeast through Sallisaw, Oklahoma and Van Buren, Arkansas. From there, it was a straight shot into North Little Rock and the two-mile jaunt across the Arkansas River into Little Rock. At Little Rock, connections could be made with Missouri Pacific Bus Lines for the 53-mile trip to the spas and racetracks at Hot Springs.

In the early 1940's, MoPac operated two pairs of trains between Kansas City and Little Rock. Trains 117-124 were the overnight *Rainbow Specials*. Their daylight counterparts were Trains 125-104. Southbound, No. 125 was known as the *Southerner*. Northbound, Train No. 116 operated as the *Southerner*, and carried sleepers, coaches, a parlor-diner, and a divided grill coach between New Orleans, Alexandria, and Little Rock. No. 104, which did not connect with No. 116, was nameless between Little Rock and Kansas City.

Southbound, the *Rainbow* departed Kansas City at 9:50pm, with an 11:00am arrival in Little Rock. Northbound, No. 124 departed Little Rock at 4:45pm and arrived in Kansas City at 7:15 the following morning. *Rainbow* consists included head-end cars, coaches, a diner-

parlor between Little Rock and Coffeyville, Kansas, and a 12 section - 1 drawing room Pullman.

Daytime *Southerner* No. 125 departed Kansas City at 8:00am and arrived in Little Rock at 9:45pm. Train 104 on the return leg departed Little Rock at 8:20am and arrived in Kansas City at 9:15pm. Included in the consists of both trains were coaches, a diner-parlor, and the Denver-Little Rock sleeper handled west of Geneseo, Kansas in the consist of the *Scenic Limited*.

Like second-string trains operating on other railroads, both the *Southerner* and the *Rainbow* came to relatively early ends. By the end of 1943, Train No. 104 had been combined in the timetable with No. 116. This simplified the task of keeping the train names straight, even though connecting service was all that was available at Little Rock. In 1948, the *Southerners* lost their parlor-diners in favor of a lightweight coach-grill-lounge, and in January, 1949, the trains were discontinued altogether.

The *Rainbows* continued to operate on their original overnight schedules for a few years longer. In 1950, the 12-1 sleeper was replaced by a 10-1-2, which itself was dropped in March, 1954, ending through sleeping car service on the route.

For a few years after that, a streamlined 10 roomette - 5 double bedroom St. Louis-Wichita Pullman was handled by the *Rainbow* between Kansas City and Durand, Kansas, where it connected with Pleasant Hill-Wichita locals 425-426. Between Kansas City and St. Louis, the Wichita car was handled by Trains 9-10, the overnight *Missourians*.

In 1950, the Coffeyville-Kansas City parlor-diner was replaced by a grill coach. Because of the extra seating space it provided, the grill coach was extended in 1953 to Kansas City-Little Rock service, thereby allowing the elimination of a full coach.

As ridership continued to decline, the railroad decided both the extra seats and the food service were surplus, and in 1956, the grill coach was withdrawn. By that time, the *Rainbow's* schedule had been switched from an overnight to a daylight run. New running times were 8:30am-11:00pm southbound, and 8:10am-11:00pm northbound.

This change, in effect, turned the train into a reincarnation of the *Southerner*, which had been discontinued several years earlier. With minor adjustments, this was the train's schedule for the rest of its operating life. Power for the *Rainbow* in its later years was usually a single EMD E-unit or an 8000-series Alco PA.

Based on claimed annual losses of more than $146,000 in 1958, Missouri Pacific petitioned the Interstate Commerce Commission in October, 1959 for permission to drop the train. The railroad's brief, filed in February, 1960, is instructive.

Among other things, MoPac cited an average total daily passenger load of 41, as well as competition by highways, bus lines and the Frisco Railroad. Several important shippers lent their support to the application, expressing the belief that reduced passenger losses would result in lower freight rates.

In opposition, local citizens worried that losing the trains would interrupt mail service, or would make it harder to ship time-sensitive commodities like milk and cream. Funeral director Thomas Dangers of Ozark, Arkansas fretted that he shipped and received "approximately 15 bodies a year on Missouri Pacific," and that if he had to transport them by ambulance or hearse instead, his costs would increase significantly. The ICC was unmoved. Following hearings in Coffeyville and Fort Smith, permission to drop the service was granted and the *Rainbow Specials* rattled off their last miles on March 29, 1960.

Right: Last call! That tad standing at the right seems intent on committing every detail to memory as the *Rainbow Special* calls for the last time at Sallisaw, Oklahoma on a balmy March 29, 1960. Northbound Train 126 has already departed for Kansas City, so this will be the last scheduled passenger train over the line. *Gordon Mott photo, Louis Marre collection*

Above: Looks like the hogger has PA-3 8030 in the company notch as the *Rainbow* pounds across the bridge at Frog Bayou, near Alma, Arkansas on September 13, 1958. Did any branch line passenger train ever look sharper? *Louis Marre*

Below: Passenger geep 4137 leads the two-car northbound remnant of the *Southern Scenic* out of the bore at Cricket Tunnel, Arkansas on a sunny morning in October, 1958. By this time, the train was obviously coach-only and had been cut back to a Pleasant Hill-Newport run. Chances are, even with a single coach, there was plenty of space available for everybody aboard. *Wayne Leeman photo, Charlie Duckworth collection*

The *Delta Eagle*

Perhaps the most unconventional entry in Missouri Pacific's *Eagle* fleet made its inaugural run on Sunday, May 11, 1941, when Train No. 334, the northbound *Delta Eagle* pulled out of Tallulah, Louisiana bound for Memphis, Tennessee. Departing at 6:15am, the run consumed five hours and forty minutes covering the 259 miles between the two Mississippi River ports.

Once reaching Memphis Union Station, the train was turned, and returned to Tallulah as Train 335. Departure time was 4:15pm, which allowed passengers a four hour and twenty minute layover for shopping, business or sight-seeing in the big city.

The *Delta Eagle* could claim distinction in that it was the first *Eagle* to operate south of St. Louis. Further, it was the only *Eagle* to run over what amounted to a branch line, and that served only a single major population center. Unhap-

pily, it was also the first *Eagle* to disappear from the scene, making its last complete trip over the route in 1954, a brief thirteen years after its maiden run.

Similar to the process which had been used to develop the name for the original *Eagle*, Missouri Pacific employees were once again asked to suggest a suitable prefix name for the new train. In this instance, a prefix was all that was needed. That future streamliners would all be *Eagles* of some kind had been decided in 1940.

The name first adopted was the *Dixie Eagle*, but this was soon changed to the *Delta Eagle*. The new name reflected the character of the area served, which was known at the time as "Delta Country." In addition, it was believed that MoPac wished to avoid confusion with the trains of the L&N-NC&StL, which already operated a number of trains having "*Dixie*" as a prefix name.

Although the route from Memphis to Tallulah might seem a curious choice for a million-dollar, premium-service streamliner, it was actually a very safe bet. To begin with, the

area was densely populated due to a large number of farms and cotton plantations along the train's route.

For another thing, the portion of the run between Helena and McGehee was exceedingly swampy and not well served by hard surfaced roads. Finally, the *Delta Eagle* faced no direct competition from any other comparable service. For this reason, it was expected that the train would be well patronized by wealthy growers in the area. The railroad's projections proved to be correct, as the train's original investment was repaid from operating profits in a little more than four years.

Below: The original *Delta Eagle*, pictured at Marianna, Arkansas in July, 1941. That "E6" on the point is actually the one-of-a-kind 1,000 horsepower AA6, which was built with a single 567 prime mover and a 19-1/2 foot baggage room inside its streamlined carbody. *Joe Collias collection*

Missouri Pacific

—— The Delta Eagle
—— The Houstonian and Orleanean
—— The Valley Eagle and connections

mak map - 1995

More compact than the six-car original *Eagle* and the full-length, full-service *Colorado Eagle*, the *Delta Eagle's* equipment consisted of a single pair of streamlined cars, plus, during wartime, one "Eagle-ized" heavyweight coach to handle overflow traffic.

The streamlined cars were RPO-coach no. 760 (lot 1708) and grill coach no. 732 (lot 1709). Both were built in late 1940 and early 1941 by St. Louis Car Company at its north St. Louis plant. Because of the out-and-back nature of the operation, only one train set was needed to protect the schedule. Consistent with Missouri Pacific practice, neither of the cars were named.

RPO-coach 760 had an inside length of 78 feet, and contained a 15-foot mail compartment with distributing tables and lettercase in the end nearest the locomotive. A bulkhead with a creep door separated the RPO compartment from the two restrooms and the 60-seat "Colored" coach section.

Grill coach 732 included a lunch counter with a stainless steel kitchen, two "spacious" lounge rooms, and coach seating for 48 "White" passengers. The grill had two tables for four at the first two rows of coach seats, and stools for three at the counter. Eat-at-your-seat tray service was also offered.

Despite the segregated nature of the train, the seating accommodations in both cars were of equal quality. Each included blue, deep pile carpeting and deluxe reclining seats, blue-gray walls, and yellow ceilings. Windows were accented with Venetian blinds and hand-loomed drapes.

A cast aluminum eagle and electric clocks were mounted on the cars' bulkheads. Other amenities included individually-controlled reading lamps above each pair of seats, ash trays in the car side walls between each pair of seats and piped-in radio reception. Both cars were air-conditioned.

The exterior color scheme of the coaches was identical to the earlier *Eagle* equipment, including the bands of polished aluminum above and below the windows. However, the full-width diaphragms found on the St. Louis-Kansas City trains were not used, and the rear coach had a conventional vestibule rather than a tapered end. The *Delta Eagle* cars were built from a low-alloy, high tensile steel, instead of aluminum. This made the *Delta* cars about 20,000 pounds heavier than comparable cars for the original *Eagle*.

An unusual element of the train was its motive power. Instead of the conventional E3's

purchased for the *Missouri River Eagle* or the E6's that subsequently powered the *Colorado Eagle*, MoPac specified the one-of-a-kind EMD "AA6" for the new *Delta Eagle*. Delivered in 1940 as Missouri Pacific 7100, the 1,000 horse-power AA6 was essentially a standard E6 equipped with a single V-12 prime mover and a single A1A powered truck instead of the usual two. In the spot where the second diesel was otherwise located was a 19-1/2 foot baggage room.

Conceptually, no. 7100 was similar to Rock Island's pair of AB units that powered the Colorado Springs section of the *Rocky Mountain Rocket*. Externally, however, the MoPac unit featured a streamlined cab instead of the boxcab styling of Rock Island's AB's. Underpowered for anything other than branchline or light mainline duty, the AA6 was retired in February, 1962, and was scrapped.

In preparation for the new train's introduction, extra section gangs were mobilized to upgrade the Memphis-Tallulah route. Low rail joints were raised, new ballast was laid and new ties were installed. In low-lying areas, drag lines were used to reinforce embankments. As a result of the extra track work, top speeds over the route were raised to between 50 and 65 mph. Plans called for the *Delta Eagle* to be refueled during the overnight layover at Tallulah; running repairs would be performed as part of the turnaround operation in Memphis.

Shortly before the start of scheduled operations, the *Delta Eagle* equipment was dispatched

Below: RPO-coach 760 and grill coach 732 constituted the entire *Delta Eagle* consist. Consistent with social customs of the time in the south, the 60-seat forward coach was designated for "Colored" passengers and the 48-seat trailing coach for "Whites." Decor and seating quality in both cars, however, were equally plush. *St. Louis Car Company photo, Charlie Duckworth collection*

on a ten-day exhibition tour. The tour actually paid its own way, as numerous "Good-will" riders from surrounding towns traveled into Memphis to sample the ride.

Many people living in the area turned out to inspect the new equipment, although response from Black residents was at first disappointing. Sadly, reflecting the realities of the time, the reason was that most Blacks believed that they "would not be permitted to ride [any train] so grand and shiny," and so simply did not bother to turn out. To its credit, the railroad responded quickly to dispel the erroneous notion.

On the morning of April 30th, the *Eagle* paid a "courtesy call" at Little Rock, where state and MoPac officials boarded the train for the inaugural run. At the first stop in Wynne, 1,400 well-wishers inspected the cars.

The next stop was at Marianna for a luncheon, and to pick up 100 citizens who rode the train to Tallulah for more festivities and a barbecue. Over the next several days, the *Delta Eagle* was displayed at Marianna, Helena, Elaine, Snow Lake, Watson and Lake Village. Finally, the train was returned to Memphis for the commencement of operations the following day.

Once in operation, the southbound *Delta Eagle* departed Memphis Union Station and crossed the Chicago-New Orleans main line of the Illinois Central Railroad. For a time, the crossing was protected by an ordinary red-yellow-green traffic signal hung over the tracks.

After bridging the Mississippi River, the *Delta Eagle* traveled over the former Iron Mountain line along the west bank of the river through Marianna, Helena and McGehee, Arkansas. At McGehee, it crossed over to the rails of the former Little Rock, Mississippi River & Texas, another Iron Mountain predecessor acquired by Jay Gould in 1887.

From McGehee, the line headed directly south through Lake Village and Eudora where it entered the state of Louisiana for the final 48-mile run into Tallulah. A Missouri Pacific Trailways bus connection at Lake Village provided service into Greenville, Mississippi. MoPac Trailways bus service was also available on a separate schedule from Monroe, Arkansas to Natchez, Mississippi.

Apart from the *Delta Eagle*, the only other passenger service along the route was a pair of doodlebugs running between Memphis and Helena, Arkansas as Trains 331-330, and a second pair between McGehee and Vidalia, Louisiana as Trains 341-342. From Vidalia, bus connections were available into Natchez.

Further north, motor trains 841-840 off the Clarendon branch connected with the *Eagle* at Helena. Daily-except-Sunday mixed train service was also available between Clarendon and Barton Junction. Not surprisingly, none of these skimpy offerings survived to mid-century. By 1944, the McGehee-Vidalia doodlebug had been replaced by a bus. The Memphis-Helena jobs were dropped in January, 1948. Passenger service over the Clarendon branch was discontinued at the beginning of 1949.

An important connection for the *Delta Eagle* was at McGehee, Arkansas. There, the *Eagles* exchanged passengers with Trains 116-103, a pair of overnighters that offered coach, grill-coach and 12-1 Pullman service between Little

Below: Looks like the *Eaglette* motor train is taking the day off, as AA6 7100 and a single combine car load baggage and express at the depot in Helena, Arkansas. By the date of this October, 1958 photo, the original *Delta Eagle* schedule had been cut back to a Helena-McGehee run. Operations ceased altogether in February, 1960. *Wayne Leeman photo, Kevin EuDaly collection*

Rock and Alexandria, Louisiana, with connections via the T&P to New Orleans.

Interestingly, although they were never anything more than secondary operations, 103 and 116 nevertheless managed to outlast the *Delta Eagles* by five years, not making their final runs until October 1, 1959. In a year when Missouri Pacific claimed its passenger service lost more than $17 million on a fully allocated basis, and $6.1 million in direct costs, the savings resulting from dropping the two trains amounted to $168,000.

The first changes came for the *Delta Eagle* in 1943, when departure times were changed from 6:15am northbound and 4:30pm southbound to 5:20am and 4:15pm respectively. Northbound departures changed in 1944 to 5:00am and then to 4:30am in 1950. Southbound departure time was advanced to 4:00pm in 1948.

In January, 1952, the schedule was cut back to Memphis-McGehee, and in 1954 cut again between Helena and Memphis, with this segment replaced by a bus connection. At the same time, the name *Delta Eagle* was dropped from the timetable, and the locomotive-drawn consist

was replaced by rebuilt *Eaglette* no. 670, which had previously worked the Union-Lincoln connection with the *Missouri River Eagle*. The 97-mile Helena-McGehee segment hung on until February 27, 1960, when the *Eaglette* was discontinued, ending passenger service over the route.

The *Valley Eagle*

Seven years after the introduction of the *Delta Eagle*, and 600 miles to the southwest of the *Delta's* route, Missouri Pacific rolled out the last of its new, postwar streamliners. The date was October 31, 1948. The train was the *Valley Eagle*, the second new *Eagle* to enter the fleet in 1948. Like the earlier *Delta* and *Missouri River Eagles*, the *Valley Eagle* was a short-haul, daylight operation. Singularly, however, it was the only *Eagle* to operate entirely within the boundaries of a single state.

The main stem of the *Valley Eagle* was between Houston and Brownsville, the southernmost U.S. city on the Texas-Mexico border. Operating as Gulf Coast Lines (St. Louis, Brownsville & Mexico) Nos. 11-12, the *Valley*

Eagle also forwarded a through St. Louis-Corpus Christi coach from No. 21, the "South" *Texas Eagle*.

Also in the consist was a San Antonio-Brownsville coach that was handled north of Corpus Christi by Trains 205-206 over the San Antonio, Uvalde and Gulf (known familiarly as the "Sausage Line"). The St. Louis-Corpus Christi coach, which was the longest through-car operation on the railroad at 1,183 miles, was handed off to No. 205 at Odem for the final 17 miles of its run. Southbound connections between Corpus Christi and Brownsville were also available at Robstown via Missouri Pacific Bus Lines.

Southbound, the *Valley Eagle* departed Houston at 10:45am, which permitted a 45-minute connection with No. 21-201 from St.

The First Streamliner?

Like many large passenger-carrying railroads, Missouri Pacific at one time operated an extensive fleet of self-propelled gas-electric motorcars on its main lines and secondary branches. Known popularly as "doodlebugs," these cars prowled numerous low-density MoPac routes from the 1920's until they were retired in the late 1940's and early 1950's.

A unique entry in the motor train fleet arrived on the scene in 1933, when the Texas & Pacific purchased streamlined power car no. 100 and trailer coach no. 150 from the Budd Company. It was perhaps the strangest piece of equipment the railroad ever owned-so much so, that for many years after its brief career came to an end, the T&P refused to admit ever having owned it.

The story of no. 100 actually began in 1930 when the Budd Company, searching for an attention-getting way to break into the railcar market, began tinkering with a new stainless steel alloy called "18-8" (18% chromium and 8% nickel added to high-grade carbon steel) as a material for building passenger equipment.

The new compound proved to be a bona-fide breakthrough: Tensile strength exceeded 150,000 pounds per square inch with a compression factor of more than 500,000 pounds. In layman's terms, it meant that railroad cars could be built with 18-8 stainless that was half the thickness of standard steel, with no loss of strength. Budd wasted no time building a prototype.

To further differentiate its pride and joy from more conventional equipment, Budd decided that the cars would roll on rubber tires, rather than standard steel wheels. In this, Budd was not the innovator; the original idea had come from France, where Michelin had developed a rubber railroad tire that was meeting with some success.

Budd, which had already acquired a reputation as an innovator, obtained from Michelin a license for Goodyear Tire & Rubber to make the tires in the United States. With rights to the necessary technology secured, the Budd Company was off to the races.

Budd's first effort was Car 65, which was purchased by the Reading Company in 1932 for use on its commuter branch line between Hatboro and New Hope, Pennsylvania. The car measured 50 feet in length and weighed 12 tons.

Naturally, it was constructed of shotwelded, fluted stainless steel. No. 65 was powered by a 125-horsepower Cummins diesel connected to a General Electric generator. The car rode on six-wheeled trucks, with traction motors on the rear truck only. As advertised, a Goodyear tire inflated to 100 PSI

was mounted on each of the twelve wheels. The car carried 47 passengers and could travel at speeds up to 47 MPH.

To say Car 65 was a disaster would be putting it charitably. In addition to frequent mechanical breakdowns and tire blowouts, it was soon discovered that the springy tires actually caused the wheels to bounce off the rails. Within a few years, Reading was fed up with its white elephant, and stored the car at its Wayne Junction shops in Philadelphia. It was cut up for scrap at the beginning of World War II.

The next purchaser of Budd-Michelin railcars was the Pennsylvania Railroad, which bought a paired power car and trailer in 1932. Except for their Tuscan red exteriors, the cars were identical to the one owned by Reading. As it turned out, Pennsy's experience with the Budds was also less than satisfactory, with frequent derailments and breakdowns the rule rather than the exception.

Blessed with greater resources than the smaller Reading, however, PRR had more of a never-say-die attitude about its equipment, and in 1936 rebuilt the cars with 30-inch steel wheels and gas-electric power. In their new configuration, the Budds performed more or less satisfactorily on the Pennsy until 1948, when they were sold to the Washington and Old Dominion. The cars were finally retired in 1953.

Budd's grandest effort - and most spectacular failure - took place in 1933, when it delivered

cars 100 and 150 to the Texas & Pacific. Unlike the Reading and Pennsy equipment, the T&P cars were no lowly commuter conveyances. Power car 100 weighed 40 tons and was powered by a pair of 240-horsepower, 12-cylinder American-LaFrance gasoline engines. Packed into No. 100's nearly 70-foot length were an engine room, a Mail-RPO section and a baggage room. Because its relatively heavy weight could not be supported by pneumatic tires, no. 100 was built with two four-wheeled power trucks equipped with conventional steel wheels.

Trailer car no. 150 was slightly more than 69 feet long and contained coach seating for 76. No. 150 weighed only 12 tons, however, and thus was able to run with - you guessed it - pneumatic tires, 16 of them, in fact. The car was appointed with deep blue upholstered seats, indirect lighting, Formica wall paneling, carpeted aisles and a fully carpeted, 16 seat "observation lounge."

The complete train, christened "*Silver Slipper*," was finished in natural stainless steel. In deference to the Southwest's brutal summer heat, it was equipped with air conditioning, and was geared for 75 MPH running.

With its nearly full-length equipment, heavier weight and more complete amenities, *Silver Slipper* was conceptually very similar to Burlington's Budd-built *Zephyr* of 1934. In that regard, the train could perhaps lay claim to being the country's first streamlined passenger train.

The *Slipper's* initial assignment was the 245-mile run between Ft. Worth and Texarkana over the secondary main line through Paris and Sherman, Texas.

Sadly, *Silver Slipper* never turned a wheel in regularly scheduled service. On its initial publicity run, one of coach 150's wheels separated from its axle and bounced away into the trackside weeds. Subsequent trial runs proved no more successful.

Coach 150 refused to stay on the tracks, the front truck on power car 100 repeatedly overheated and the American-LaFrance engines conked out over and over again. Worse, during summer weather the air conditioning was badly overmatched, so that the temperature inside the coach could not be coaxed below 90 degrees.

The T&P tried its best. After monkeying with various sizes and types of tires for the coach, the railroad gave up and replaced the rubber tires with conventional trucks. It didn't help. Because of the car's light weight relative to its springing, the hard steel wheels caused it to ride like a buckboard on a back-country road.

A year after its arrival on the property, the gleaming silver train still could not be made to operate properly, and in fact had failed to earn a single revenue dollar. Worse, it had consumed an inordinate amount of scarce, Depression-era cash in the form of repair time and materials.

In late 1934, T&P President John L. Lancaster finally called it quits, banishing the

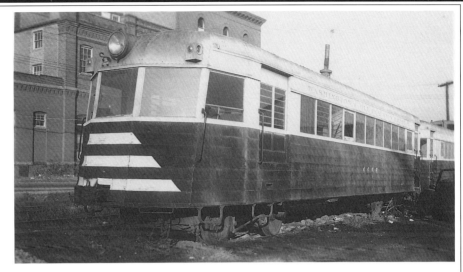

Above: Here's Washington & Old Dominion Budd car 4688 and trailer 4689 near the end of their careers, and after having their pneumatic tires and Cummins diesels replaced by steel wheels and a gas- electric power plant.

Silver Slipper to the storage tracks. As historian Bert Pennypacker describes the situation, "The strong-willed Lancaster wasn't a man to accept defeat easily; and because of this, T&P for a number of years denied the one-time existence of a Budd-Michelin train on its property."

It had been there, all right; you just had to know where to look.

The cars were sold by original owner Pennsy to the W&OD in 1948 and repainted from Tuscan red to the black and gray shown in this photo. *Ed Keilty collection*

Below: T&P's "Silver Slipper" consisted of Budd power car 100 and trailer coach 150. Despite their advanced design, the units proved too temperamental for the rigors of service in the hot climate of East Texas. Without ever turning a wheel in revenue service, the shiny equipment was consigned to the scrap line and was never heard of again. *Bert Pennypacker collection, courtesy* Trains *magazine*

Above: Wouldn't this be a great train to model? Train 304, the New Orleans-Houston *Orleanean* pauses at the depot in Baton Rouge, Louisiana in the summer of 1961. The heavy-weight consist has been completely rebuilt and modernized, and looks every bit as sharp as any of her streamlined sisters. *Harold K. Vollrath collection*

Right: Big-as-a-barn PA-3 8034 idles impatiently at Brownsville, Texas with Gulf Coast Lines Train 316, the overnight *Houstonian*. Included in the consist are reclining seat coaches and a modernized 8-5 heavyweight Pullman. *Harold K. Vollrath collection*

Bottom: It's a good thing it's summertime in Texas, because StLB&M F3 545 is a freight unit, and thus not equipped with a steam generator to warm the cars. The 1,500 horsepower unit leads the *Valley Eagle* at Odem on August 25, 1958. *Joe McMillan*

Louis and Memphis. Connection with No. 205 from San Antonio at Odem was at 3:35pm. Arrival in Brownsville was at 7:40pm, for an average speed over the 371-mile route of slightly better than 40 mph. On the return trip, *Valley Eagle* No. 12 left Brownsville at 6:45am. Arrival in Houston was at 3:15pm, again allowing a 45 minute connection with *Texas Eagle* 202-22. The connection at Odem with Train 206 was at 10:20am. Arrival in San Antonio for No. 206 was at 1:55pm.

The consist for Nos. 11-12 included coaches and a grill coach between Houston and Brownsville, plus the St. Louis-Corpus Christi and San Antonio-Brownsville coaches. Lightweight equipment was built by American Car and Foundry in 1948 as part of an order for 69 streamlined chair, food service and head end cars for MoPac's new Texas trains. Forty-seven new sleepers from Pullman-Standard were delivered at the same time.

The ten cars designated for *Valley Eagle* service included six unique-on-the-system "deluxe coaches with stateroom" nos. 850-855, built as ACF lot no. 2906. The other *Valley* cars were mail-baggage nos. 816-817 (ACF lot no. 2904) and divided grill coaches 824-825 (ACF lot no. 2905). Because these were segregated coaches operating in the Deep South, the grill section was positioned in the center of the car, thereby forming the divider between the "Colored" and "White" sections. Power for the trains, especially in later years, varied, but likely started out as EMD E7 units 7008-7009, delivered in 1947. Other diesel passenger power assigned to the StLB&M included EMD F7 units 611-616 and GP7's 4323 and 4324, delivered in 1950 and 1954. All were equipped with steam generators and geared for high-speed passenger service.

Because the *Valley Eagle* was entirely a Gulf Coast Lines operation, both the cars and the E7's were originally assigned to (and sublettered for) subsidiary StLB&M. The sets stayed together for only a short time, however, before individual cars found their way into other service on the *Texas Eagle* and other MoPac trains. All the *Valley Eagle* cars were retired between 1967 and 1970.

Companion trains for the *Valley Eagle* over the Houston-Brownsville route were StLB&M Trains 15-16, the overnight *Pioneers*. These trains offered coach and 10-1-2 Pullman service between Houston-Brownsville and Houston-Corpus Christi, with a bus connection to Mission, Texas. Southbound, No. 15 operated on a 9:20pm-8:00am schedule; northbound, departure and arrival times were 8:15pm-7:30am. Arrival and departure at Corpus Christi were 4:35am and 11:45pm, respectively.

With only minor schedule variations, operating patterns for the *Valley Eagle* remained unchanged into the 1950's. The first major alterations came in the mid-50's, when the timetable numbers were changed from 11-12 to 321-322. In June, 1956, Trains 205-206 were discontinued, ending through service between San Antonio and Brownsville.

Two years later, in September, 1958, the St. Louis-Corpus Christi through coach was dropped. After that, passengers bound from St. Louis to Gulf Coast points beyond Houston had to rely on an across-the-platform connection rather than through-car service.

The final change took place in 1961, when the departure time for No. 321 was moved from 11:30am to 12:15pm, with an arrival time in Brownsville at 9:10pm. The *Valley Eagles* made their final departures on July 1, 1962. At the time, the railroad claimed to be losing more than $131,000 per year on the operation.

Changes for the overnight *Pioneer* were also gradual. At the same time the *Valley Eagle's* numbers were changed, the Pioneer's numbers were also changed to 315-316. In 1953, the second Houston-Brownsville Pullman was dropped. The remaining sleeper was changed in 1957, first to an 8-1-2, and then to an 8-5.

In 1961, the Pullman was upgraded a final time, to one of the original 6-6-4's built for the 1942 *Colorado Eagle*. At about the same time,

timetable numbers for the train were changed again, to 55-54. Sleeping car service was dropped altogether at the end of January, 1964.

MoPac's handling of the *Pioneer* during its final years of operation was distressingly similar to its inept disposition of the *Colorado Eagle* discontinuance. Whether the Dearmont-Jenks administration preferred playing hardball or simply had a tin ear for public relations may never be known, but the technique was familiar and the result a foregone conclusion.

First, like the *Colorado Eagle*, the train lost its sleepers and was downgraded to coach-only status. Next, the schedule was revised to make riding the train as inconvenient as possible, in this case by advancing (and for once, speeding up) the northbound operation from 8:45pm-7:00am to an unattractive 6:45pm-3:30am carding.

In 1965, it was changed again, to 6:01pm-2:33am. By this time, average ridership was down to five or six per trip, and MoPac asked the Texas Railroad Commission for permission to call it quits.

Reaction to the railroad's petition was hardly surprising. In an article in the Brownsville Herald, Chamber of Commerce President Glen Herman fumed that, "If passengers were not confronted with absurd schedules, indifferent or surly personnel, hidden passenger terminals and Gay 90's (sic) equipment, they would be more willing to ride the railroad."

MoPac was also criticized in the Corpus Christi Caller for crawfishing on a promise made only a year earlier to maintain passenger service in the Rio Grande Valley. As a means of reducing operating expenses, there was even a proposal to replace the train's conventional equipment with Budd Rail Diesel Cars in an expanded service. Missouri Pacific wasn't about to bite on that, however, and with ridership scraping bottom, there wasn't much of a case to be made for keeping the trains in operation.

Right: In 1948, St. Louis, Brownsville & Mexico took delivery on "deluxe coaches with stateroom" 850-855 for the *Valley Eagle* streamliner. Here, no. 850 poses outside ACF's St. Charles, Missouri plant in September, 1948. Within a month, she'll be open for business between Houston and the Mexican border. *ACF photo, Alan Wayne Hegler collection*

Above: It's hard to tell where the consist of *Houstonian* No. 52 ends and the next train begins in this photo taken at New Orleans in April, 1963. That lightweight sleeper bringing up the markers is a 14-1-2 car built by Pullman-Standard in 1948. *J. W. Swanberg*

After the usual hearings, the Commission bowed to the inevitable and granted the railroad's petition for discontinuance. Nameless in the timetable, Trains 55 and 54 made their final runs on the night of March 16, 1966, bringing to an end all railroad passenger service in the Rio Grande Valley.

The *Houstonian* and *Orleanean*

At the time it was acquired by the Missouri Pacific in 1925, the Gulf Coast Lines consisted of three predecessor companies. These were the St. Louis, Brownsville & Mexico, between Houston and Brownsville, Texas, the Beaumont, Sour Lake & Western, between Houston and Beaumont, and the New Orleans, Texas & Mexico.

As originally planned, the NOT&M was to run from Beaumont to Baton Rouge with extensions to Memphis and New Orleans. By September, 1909, construction had been completed on a line down the west shore of the Mississippi River from Anchorage, Louisiana, opposite Baton Rouge, to DeQuincy, near the Texas border. Trackage rights between Beaumont and DeQuincy over the Kansas City Southern were obtained at about the same time, ending the need for further construction on the Beaumont line.

Gulf Coast Lines' passenger service into the Crescent City commenced on September 1, 1909, with the completion of a trackage rights agreement with the Illinois Central. This al-

lowed the GCL to operate between Baton Rouge and New Orleans over the IC-controlled Louisiana Railway & Navigation Company. In exchange, the proposed Memphis line and the New Orleans extension, both of which would have competed directly with the IC's Memphis-to-New Orleans main line, were never built.

Interestingly, the GCL (and later, the Missouri Pacific) and the Illinois Central enjoyed a close relationship in New Orleans. Gulf Coast Lines power and equipment were serviced at IC's downtown Government Yard, and IC crews operated GCL trains between New Orleans and Baton Rouge. IC conductors and trainmen actually wore Missouri Pacific uniforms, and the New Orleans Union Passenger Terminal timetables listed GCL trains under both Missouri Pacific and Illinois Central numbers as "Baton Rouge Trains."

In the 1930's, the NOT&M operated two pairs of trains over the 367-mile line between New Orleans and Houston. These were the daylight *Orleanean* and the overnight *Houstonian*.

Trains 3-4, the *Orleanean*, carried deluxe coaches, chair cars, an observation-parlor-diner and a 12-1 Pullman from Los Angeles that was handled west of Houston by the Santa Fe. Westbound, departure from New Orleans was at 9:50am, with arrival in Houston at 8:20pm. Eastbound running times were 8:20am-7:15pm. Intermediate stops included Baton Rouge,

Opelousas, Kinder, DeQuincy, and Beaumont. Arrival in Los Angeles for the through sleeper was at 7:30am the third morning out.

Eastbound, the Los Angeles Pullman departed at 10:45pm, arriving in New Orleans at 7:15pm the third night out. To gauge the success of the through Pullman operation, compare the MP-Santa Fe times with that of Southern Pacific's competing *Sunset Limited*, which, in the 1940's, made the New Orleans-Los Angeles run in a flat 48 hours (eventually trimmed to 42).

Overnight Houston-New Orleans service was protected by *Houstonians* 9-10, which fielded coaches, a 10-section observation-sleeper, and a 12-1 Pullman between Houston and Monroe, Louisiana, that was handled north of Kinder by Missouri Pacific Train 115, the *Southerner*. Westbound, Train 9 departed New Orleans at 9:15pm and arrived in Houston at 7:45am. Eastbound, No. 10 left Houston at

9:30pm and arrived in New Orleans at 7:40am. Average speed over the route was slightly more than 35 mph, about average for secondary trains of the era.

Except for minor schedule and consist changes, operations for both trains remained fairly constant for most of their lives. By the 1940's, *Orleaneans* had been renumbered twice, first to 5-6 and then back to 3-4 again. The New Orleans-Los Angeles Pullman was rerouted to Oakland, with connections into San Francisco.

Other changes included the substitution of a straight parlor car for the observation car in 1944, and the discontinuance of the west coast sleeper in 1943 in favor of a New Orleans-Corpus Christi Pullman that was handled south of Houston in the consist of GCL No. 15, the *Pioneer*.

The Oakland sleeper returned in 1950, this time as a 6-6-4 car that was once more forwarded west in the consist of Santa Fe Trains 23-24, the *Grand Canyon*. In 1954, the sleeper was changed a final time to an 8-section, 2-compartment, 2-drawing room car, which it remained until it was eliminated altogether in May, 1956.

Night trains 9-10 exchanged their 12-1 Pullmans for 8-5 cars after 1948, and lost their food service cars about the same time. The sleeper was changed again in June, 1959 to a heavyweight 8-6-1-1 car, and then in May, 1960 to another heavyweight 12-1-4 car. Lightweight sleepers finally arrived in April, 1961, when the 12-1-4 Pullman was upgraded to a 14-1-2 car.

In 1957, the Gulf Coast Lines trains were again renumbered. Under the revised scheme, Nos. 3-4 became 303-304 and Nos. 9-10 were changed to 309-310. This changed again in 1962, consistent with the general renumbering system-wide. At that time, 303-304 were changed to Nos. 51 westbound and 50 eastbound, and Nos. 309-310 were changed to Nos. 53 westbound and 52 eastbound. Both train pairs continued to use these timetable numbers until their eventual discontinuance in the mid-1960's.

By the 1960's, the former Gulf Coast flyers had become mere shadows of their former full-service selves. In January, 1964, the *Orleanean's* parlor car was dropped, and replaced by a grill coach that lasted only until April 30.

After that, the *Orleanean* operated on a nine hour and fifteen minute schedule with no food or beverage service whatsoever. Trains 51-50, now nameless in the timetable, made their final runs on March 11, 1965. By this time, they were down to a single streamlined coach trailing a Geep and a handful of head-end cars.

The *Houstonians* lasted a little longer, although with few of their original amenities still intact. The 14-1-2 Pullmans added in 1961 remained in the consists until February, 1964, when sleeper service on the route was discontinued. The *Houstonian* was down to one or two coaches plus a cut of mail and express cars, hardly a consist likely to attract a great deal of overnight ridership. It was in this form that nameless Nos. 53-52 made their last runs on the night of May 25, 1967.

Below: It's wall-to-wall action as *Orleaneans* 51 and 50 meet at Eunice, Louisiana in early 1965. Meanwhile, GP7 276 cools its heels next to Rock Island's "Little Rock" line crossing, waiting for the main line to clear so it can get back to work. *J. Parker Lamb*

9 The Chicago & Eastern Illinois

At the end of World War II, the Chicago and Eastern Illinois Railroad was operating twenty-two daily and two winter season trains over its three passenger routes between Chicago and St. Louis, southern Illinois and Evansville, Indiana, where trains for Florida, Atlanta and Gulf Coast points were handed off to the L&N. Because of the many connections made at Evansville, the line was unquestionably the most important passenger route on the railroad.

In the spring of 1946, southbound local service from Chicago to Evansville was provided by nameless Trains 1 and 9. No. 1 was a

Right: ACF-built motor cars *Salem* and *Mount Vernon* protected the schedule of Chicago & Eastern Illinois Trains 121-122, the *Egyptian Zipper* between Villa Grove and Cypress. The train's name is a reference to the area of southern Illinois known as "Little Egypt," where place-names like Cairo and Thebes abound. In this 1940 photo, the crew of car 245 poses at the station in Danville, Illinois. *Paul Moffitt photo, Ray Curl collection*

Below: Was there ever a more universal pastime than waving at trains? C&EI Train 4, the northbound "Chicago Liner" *Whippoorwill* drifts through the curve at Liberty Lane, near Danville, Illinois in July, 1947. The deep blue and gold trains operated with coaches and a diner-lounge car on a fast daylight schedule between Chicago and Evansville, Indiana. *Paul Moffitt photo, Ray Curl collection*

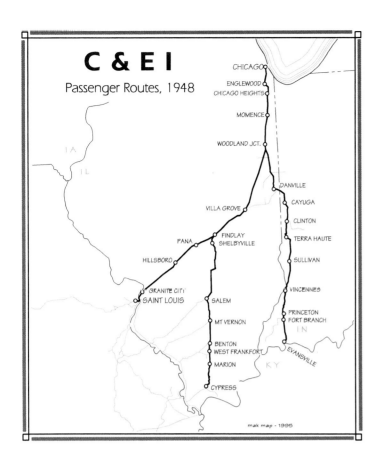

C & E I
Passenger Routes, 1948

CHICAGO
ENGLEWOOD
CHICAGO HEIGHTS
MOMENCE
WOODLAND JCT.
DANVILLE
CAYUGA
VILLA GROVE
CLINTON
FINDLAY
PANA
SHELBYVILLE
TERRA HAUTE
HILLSBORO
SULLIVAN
GRANITE CITY
SAINT LOUIS
VINCENNES
SALEM
PRINCETON
FORT BRANCH
MT VERNON
BENTON
WEST FRANKFORT
EVANSVILLE
MARION
CYPRESS

mak map - 1995

Above: The crew of Santa Fe switcher 2400 looks on admiringly as F3 1200 leads Train 81, the *Georgian* out of Chicago's famed Dearborn Station in 1948. Dearborn was the home of a number of storied flyers, including Santa Fe's *Chief* and *Super Chief*, Wabash's *Blue Bird* and *Banner Blue*, Monon's *Thoroughbred* and GTW's *Maple Leaf* and *International Limited*. *Ray Curl collection*

Below: Summer is in full flower as F3 1203 leads the southbound *Georgian* at Glenwood, Illinois in June, 1948. Note the four heavy-weight cars at the rear of the train, including three that have been modernized with blue and silver paint to match the streamlined forward section. *Paul Moffitt photo, Ray Curl collection*

Right: A heavyweight Pullman and Budd demonstrator RDC-1 bring up the markers of the northbound *Meadowlark* at Watseka, Illinois in March, 1950. Within a few years, the original four-car streamlined consist of the train would be replaced by the Budd car on the run between Chicago and Cypress, Illinois. *Robert Lewis photo, Ray Curl collection*

coach-only day train that was scheduled for an incredible 49 stops along the 287-mile route, or about one stop every six miles. Departure time for No. 1 from Chicago was at 8:30am, with arrival in Evansville at 6:35pm. Average speed was slightly less than 30 MPH, including a 25-minute lunch stop at Danville.

No. 9 was an overnight coach and sleeper operation that departed Chicago at 11:59pm and arrived in Evansville at 7:55am after seventeen positive and conditional stops. Northbound locals were 4:30pm-12:15am No. 10, which returned No. 9's sleeper to Chicago as a parlor car, and No. 8, a moderately well-equipped day train that carried coaches, a diner and a heavyweight parlor-observation. Unlike No. 1's leisurely pace, No. 8 covered the Chicago run in a comparatively snappy six hours and thirty-five minutes following its 12:30pm departure from Evansville.

Despite the fact that C&EI handled as many as sixteen trains a day between Chicago and Evansville, the primary thrust of its passenger operations was through its connection with the Louisville & Nashville. At Evansville, the two railroads handed off trains originating in Chicago, New Orleans, Atlanta and a variety of Florida cities, and returned them home again.

Of all the joint services, the most famous was the *Dixie Flyer*, Trains 95-94, which began operating between Chicago and Florida in 1892.

The *Flyer* persevered in one form or another until 1965, making it one of the longest-lived continuous train names in American railroading.

Below: The crew seems pleased to be photographed with steam generator-equipped EMD BL2 no. 200 as it poses at Villa Grove, Illinois in the spring of 1950. The train is believed to be an RPO demonstration run for the Post Office Department, and not a regularly scheduled operation. *Ray Curl collection*

The *Flyer* handled coaches to Jacksonville, a diner to Macon, Georgia, and sleepers between Chicago and Atlanta, Jacksonville, Miami, and St. Petersburg, Florida. Also in the consist was a 10-section Chicago-Jacksonville observation lounge car. Departure from Chicago was at 11:40pm with arrival in Miami at 5:10pm the second afternoon out.

Other trains on the route in 1946 were Nos. 89-88, the Chicago-New Orleans *Dixie Express*, Nos. 93-92 the Chicago-Florida *Dixie Limited*, Nos. 97-96, the Chicago-New Orleans *Dixie Mail* and Nos. 99-98, the every-third-day Chicago-Miami *Dixie Flagler*. Operating during the winter season only were Trains 87-86, the *Dixieland*. Altogether, the *Limited, Flyer, Flagler* and *Dixieland* combined to make the 925 route-mile C&EI Chicago's foremost passenger carrier to the Sunshine State.

The first streamlined train on the C&EI was the all-coach, *Dixie Flagler*, which made its inaugural run on December 17, 1940. The equipment for this train was not new, but was delivered by Budd to the Florida East Coast in 1939 for the Jacksonville-Miami *Henry M. Flagler*.

By extending the run from Jacksonville to Chicago, the train was cut back from a daily to an

Below: An all-heavyweight *Dixie Limited* drums north through Danville, Illinois late on a winter morning in 1948. The *Dixie Limited* began as a Chicago-Florida operation that was cut back to a Chicago-Evansville-Nashville routing in 1951. *Paul Moffitt photo, Ray Curl collection*

every-third-day operation. This did not eliminate daily service, however, as the *Flagler* became one of three seven-car coach trains running over separate routes on alternating, every-third-day schedules between Chicago and Miami.

With the rescheduling, Nos. 99-98 became part of a nine-railroad cooperative venture intended to recapture the vacation trade from the highways. The rest of the lineup included the *South Wind* via the Pennsylvania, L&N, Nashville, Chattanooga & St. Louis, Atlantic Coast

Above: Another look at the *Georgian* as she makes an easy 30 MPH approaching Jefferson Street in Atlanta on the morning of August 25, 1948. Despite the C&EI power on the point, the train at this point is in fact an NC&StL operation. After a two-hour layover in the Peachtree City, the Central of Georgia and ACL will forward No. 81 the rest of the way to Jacksonville. *David Salter photo, Ray Curl collection*

Above: F7 1404 and E7 1102 step carefully through the streets of Evansville with Train 92-4, the Chicago-bound *Dixie Limited* on a summer morning in 1952. The northbound *Limited* carried coaches from Jacksonville and Atlanta and a club coach from Evansville to Chicago. *C. R. Scholes*

Line and FEC, and the *City of Miami* via the Illinois Central, Central of Georgia, ACL and FEC.

The *Flagler* employed the rails of the C&EI, L&N, NC&StL, Atlanta, Birmingham & Coast, ACL, and FEC. Original C&EI power for the train was streamlined Pacific 1008. At the opposite end of the run, shiny new coral and orange EMD E3's handled the train over the FEC leg between Jacksonville and Miami.

The *Flagler* operated as a coach train until 1949, when sleepers were added between Chicago and Florida. For the 1949-50 winter season, the consist was expanded again to a full fifteen cars, including the five original Miami coaches, a Chicago-Jacksonville coach, a C&EI diner to Jacksonville and an FEC diner to Miami, a tavern-observation lounge, plus five Miami and two Jacksonville Pullmans. Also during 1949, the railroad undertook a general renumbering of its trains, so that Nos. 99-98 now appeared in the timetable as Nos. 9-10.

During the late 1940's and early 1950's, C&EI passenger trains underwent a pruning as well as an upgrading, as standard, prewar consists were replaced by a new generation of "Chicago-Liner" streamliners. The heavyweight Chicago-New Orleans *Dixie Express* was discontinued in 1947, followed by the *Dixie Mail* and the seasonal *Dixieland* in 1949. The southbound *Dixie Limited* was cut back from Chicago-Florida to Chicago-Nashville in 1951, and in 1954 the *Dixie Flagler* was replaced by the *New Dixieland*. New arrivals on the route were the streamlined Chicago-Evansville *Whippoorwill* in 1946, the Chicago-Atlanta *Georgian* in 1948 and the Chicago-New Orleans *Humming Bird* in 1952.

Prior to the delivery of streamlined equipment, C&EI trains were made up primarily of Pullman green heavyweight cars drawn by K-class USRA-type Pacifics. In 1947, the first EMD E7's arrived on the property, followed by boiler-equipped F3's in 1948. Unlike the somber Pullman green and black prewar trains, the new streamliners were painted in an attractive

orange and blue scheme that lasted until the early 1960's. In addition, several C&EI cars were painted in the dark blue, gray and gold of the L&N and were used in the equipment pool that made up the New Orleans, Atlanta, and Florida trains.

On the St. Louis and southern Illinois runs, C&EI fielded four train pairs. These were Chicago-St. Louis Nos. 21-22, the *Zipper*, and Nos. 23-24, the *Silent Knight*. Running in conjunc-

tion with the St. Louis trains were Trains 121-122, the *Egyptian Zipper* between Villa Grove and Cypress, and nameless 123-124 between Villa Grove and Thebes, Illinois.

The coach-only *Zipper* operated on an 11:45am-5:32pm schedule southbound, and a 9:35am-3:10pm schedule northbound.

The overnight *Silent Knight* offered coach and sleeping car service and operated on an 11:15pm-6:30am schedule southbound and a

Right: F-unit 1600 on the point of Train 1 rests on its side at Papineau, Illinois on July 2, 1955. Unhappily, the derailment injured 10, including one fatally. The car still upright on the rails is part of the "Chicago Liner" equipment delivered in 1947 for the *Meadowlark* and its companion *Whippoorwill*. *Ray Curl collection*

10:45pm-6:50am carding northbound. C&EI's St. Louis trains used the tracks of the Big Four (New York Central) between Pana, Illinois and St. Louis.

The *Egyptian Zipper* employed a pair of ACF-built motorcars named *Mount Vernon* and *Salem* to protect the schedule. The cars were very similar in appearance to the *Eaglette* car used on the Missouri Pacific between Lincoln and Union, Nebraska.

New in 1947 was the Chicago-Cypress *Meadowlark*, which operated on a daylight schedule with three streamlined coaches and a mail-baggage-grill combination car. This did not last long, however, as by 1955, the original diesel-powered streamliner had been replaced by a Budd RDC-1 running on a red-eye schedule that called for a 3:15am departure from Cypress. As might be expected, an operation like this was unlikely to attract much of a following, and the *Meadowlark* was eventually discontinued in 1962.

On the St. Louis route, the *Zipper* lasted only until 1947. The *Silent Knight* continued to operate until 1949. In truth, the St. Louis trains probably never stood much of a chance. Always also-rans to the better-equipped, more frequent offerings of the Wabash, Illinois Central, and Alton/GM&O, the little C&EI trains were over-matched from the outset.

Above: "Chicken-wire" F3 1202 enjoys the morning sunshine at C&EI's 51st Street Yard in Chicago in March, 1950. The F-units, plus a handful of E7's and later a single E9 formed the backbone of the road's diesel passenger fleet into the 1960's. *Paul Moffitt photo, Ray Curl collection*

Below: An impressive thirteen cars of the every-third-day *Dixie Flagler* hammer down the main line on a damp morning at Danville, Illinois in the winter of 1954. Before she reaches her final destination in Miami, the *Flagler* will travel over the rails of the C&EI, L&N, NC&StL, AB&C and the Florida East Coast. Was any other name train's operation more complex? *Ray Curl collection*

By 1960, C&EI's passenger service was down to a handful of trains, including the RDC-equipped *Meadowlark* between Chicago and Cypress, southbound Evansville local No. 1, the northbound Nashville-Chicago *Dixie Limited*, the Chicago-Jacksonville *Dixie Flyer* and the combined *Georgian-Hummingbird*, which operated over the C&EI and L&N between Chicago-St. Louis and Montgomery-Mobile-New Orleans.

Through Pullman service between Chicago and Florida ended in 1957, with the demise of the *Dixieland*. Pullman service from Chicago extended only as far as Evansville, Nashville, and Atlanta. By 1965, the *Dixie Flyer* was coach-only, as were trains 3 and 4 between Chicago and Evansville, and Nos. 1 and 92 between Danville and Evansville.

Number 93-54, the *Georgian-Hummingbird*, however, was still a full-service operation, offering Pullman and coach service between Chicago, Atlanta and Mobile, and a club-lounge-diner between Chicago and Atlanta and between Nashville and New Orleans. Coach connections between St. Louis and Evansville via the L&N continued until 1971. The C&EI's portion of the *Georgian-Hummingbird* was discontinued in 1967 after a rancorous and widely publicized series of ICC hearings.

By the time the C&EI was acquired by the Missouri Pacific, the road was down to a single passenger schedule, Trains 3 and 4 between Chicago and Evansville. Train consists included a single E7 or E9 locomotive, one or two of the Budd coaches and coach-buffet-lounge *Harvest Inn*.

Operation of this train was finally taken over by the L&N, which by ICC direction gained

Below: C&EI No. 10, the northbound *Meadowlark* tiptoes around a curve on the Westville Branch near Danville on a frosty morning in February, 1958. According to the photographer, the line between Villa Grove and Danville was strictly rated for slow speed. *J. Parker Lamb*

total ownership of the line between Evansville and Woodland Junction, and shared ownership between Woodland Junction and Chicago. Ten streamlined Budd coaches built in 1953 and numbered 475-484 became the property of the Missouri Pacific in 1967.

E9 1102 was also transferred to the MoPac and was renumbered 43. The unit remained on the property until its retirement in April, 1972. All the cars were off the roster by 1970, most having been sold back to the L&N. Trains 3 and 4 survived as L&N's unofficially-named *Danville Flyer* until Amtrak Conveyance Day in 1971.

Right: What a difference a few months make! Gone are *Meadowlark's* FP7 and streamlined consist, replaced on this December, 1958 morning by a lowly, if more economical, RDC-1. Despite the more mundane consist, however, the conductor appears to be enjoying the view from the railfan's perch in the left-hand vestibule. *J. Parker Lamb*

Below: Dressed in MoPac "Jenks blue," E7 28 powers C&EI Train 4, unofficially known as the *"Danville Flyer"* out of Dearborn Station on July 23, 1967. The train eventually became an L&N operation, running daily between Chicago and Danville until Amtrak Day in May, 1971. *Joe McMillan*

10 Headin' South - The *Texas Eagle*

No matter where you looked in 1948, the world bore only passing resemblance to what it had been a decade earlier. Two and a half years after the end of hostilities, much of Europe and the Far East was still digging out from under the wreckage of a war unprecedented in human history.

In Czechoslovakia, President Eduard Benes was forced against the popular will to install a Communist-controlled cabinet, drawing that beleaguered nation into a dark night of Soviet domination that would last for more than 40 years.

In Germany, 200 former Nazis convicted of war crimes were executed by hanging, and in Japan, a two-year trial costing $10 million was concluded as 25 military and political leaders were sentenced. In April, what came to be known as the Berlin Blockade began as Soviet military authorities interdicted a pair of Allied troop trains at the border of the Eastern Zone.

Elsewhere, amidst bitter fighting between Arabs and Jews, the new State of Israel was born on May 14. In the Vatican, Pope Pius XII declared the atomic bomb the greatest threat to mankind in the history of the world. In Wembley, England, the United States placed first in the

Below: In a book dominated by blue and gray diesels, it was hard to pass up this atmospheric photo of Mountain 5340 simmering on the head end of *Southerner* No. 7 at St. Louis Union Station in August, 1950. This photo is truly evocative of the mystique of big-time, steam-era railroading. *Donald Sims photo, Joe Collias collection*

Missouri Pacific

— The Texas Eagle
— The Louisiana Eagle
— The Aztec Eagle

mak map - 1995

Summer Olympics with a total of 662 points. And in India, a man of peace called Mohandas K. Gandhi was assassinated by political opponents.

Closer to home, a Republican-controlled Congress passed a $4.8 billion income tax cut. Tennessee Williams won the Pulitzer Prize for his play *A Streetcar Named Desire*, and novelist James Michener also won a Pulitzer for his novel *Tales of the South Pacific*.

In sports, Citation won the Triple Crown, the Cleveland Indians beat the Boston Braves four games to three to win the World Series, and Joe Louis reigned as heavyweight champ. In 1948, there were 65 licensed television stations broadcasting in the United States, including KSD in St. Louis, WGN in Chicago and WRTV in New Orleans.

Obituaries during the year included former baseball great Babe Ruth, automaker Charles

W. Nash, World War I hero General John J. Pershing, actress Carole Landis, retired Supreme Court Justice Charles Evans Hughes and comedian Edgar Kennedy. And following another difficult campaign, a now well-known Harry S. Truman defeated New York Governor Thomas Dewey for a second term as President of the United States. He would be paid $75,000 a year for his efforts.

Railroading also made news in 1948. In January, luckless Rock Island emerged from still another bankruptcy, and in May, President Truman briefly seized the country's entire railway system in anticipation of a national strike by three operating brotherhoods. Headlines of a happier nature were made later in the year with the national tour of the American Freedom Train and the opening of the Chicago Railroad Fair.

Also during 1948, a number of new or re-equipped streamliners made their debuts, in-

cluding Frisco-Katy's *Texas Special*, SP-Rock Island's *Golden State*, Santa Fe's daily *Super Chief*, New York Central's *Twentieth Century Limited*, and on August 15, 1948, Missouri Pacific's *Texas Eagle*.

In the spring of 1948, Missouri Pacific was dispatching a number of primarily steam powered and heavyweight trains over the old Iron Mountain line between St. Louis and the southwest. Mainline schedules included Nos. 3-4, the *Ozarker*, between St. Louis and Little Rock, Nos. 7-8, the mostly-mail *Southerner*, between St. Louis and Little Rock, Hot Springs, Fort Worth, Houston, and El Paso, Nos. 17-18, the *Hot Springs Special* between St. Louis and Little Rock-Hot Springs, and Nos. 25-26, the *Texan*, between St. Louis-Memphis and Fort Worth, Houston and Corpus Christi.

Connections between Memphis and Little Rock were via Trains 225-226. Local operations included Nos. 219-220, between Hot Springs and Memphis, Nos. 325-304 between Poplar Bluff, Missouri and Wynne, Arkansas, and No. 224, between Little Rock and Memphis.

The premier operation on the route was the *Sunshine Special*, a train that traced its origins to 1915. From its earliest years, the *Sunshine* was widely recognized as one of the finest trains in the country. Originally carded as Trains 1-21-201 southbound and 202-22-2 northbound, the *Sunshine* offered coach and Pullman accommodations between St. Louis and Memphis in the north and Texas, Louisiana, Mexico City, and Los Angeles in the south and west.

Consistent with its trappings as a luxury flyer, by 1931 all sections of the *Sunshine* carried lounge cars with shower-baths and, in deference to the "dry" states along the route, "soda fountains," a feature that would be continued in the new *Texas Eagle* streamlined equipment.

In the months preceding the introduction of the *Texas Eagles*, the *Sunshine Special* was operating three sections in each direction. These were Trains 1-21-31 southbound, and Trains 32-22-2 northbound. As in prior years, connecting Train 201 relayed southwest-bound sleepers between Memphis and Little Rock, where they were switched into the main stem of the *Sunshine*. Northbound, Train 226, the Memphis section of the *Texan*, handled the return cars from Little Rock.

According to the timetable, all three sections of the *Sunshine* departed St. Louis at

5:30pm. Before they reached their first stop at Tower Grove Station, however, they had already begun to space themselves out. By the time the trains reached Little Rock, No. 21 was a full 30 minutes behind No. 1; No. 31 trailed No. 21 into town 10 minutes later.

Sunshine No. 1 made positive stops at Tower Grove, Bismarck, and Poplar Bluff, Missouri, and at Hoxie, Newport, Little Rock, Gurdon, and Texarkana, Arkansas-Texas. No. 21 matched stops with No. 1, with an additional stop at Hope, Arkansas. No. 31 handled most of

Above: The last tail sign used on the *Sunshine Special* **was this one photographed at St. Louis in 1947. The sign featured a white circle, yellow sunburst and red lettering outlined in black.** *Missouri Pacific photo, Charlie Duckworth collection*

Below: T&P E7 2002 heads up *Texas Eagle* **No. 2 at Sweetwater, Texas on a winter afternoon in 1950. Looks like the streamliner has taken the hole, probably awaiting a meet with one of T&P's hotshot freights. No. 2 will be in St. Louis at 8:10am tomorrow.** *R. S. Plummer photo, Kevin EuDaly collection*

Above: Before the advent of *Eagle* blue and gray, Missouri Pacific passenger trains were Pullman green with black steam power. In the fall of 1946, Mountain 5339 powers Train 25, the southbound *Texan* at Tower Grove Station in St. Louis. The double iron in the foreground is the Frisco main to Oklahoma and Texas. *Joe Collias*

Below: Three sections of the *Sunshine Special* wait for their 5:30pm departure time at St. Louis in the late 1940's. Car assignments on Track 7 list Pullmans bound for El Dorado (car 15), Shreveport (car 17), Brownsville (car 212) and Lake Charles (car 1017). Looks like the coaches are bound for just about everywhere. *Missouri Pacific photo, Charlie Duckworth collection*

the local chores, making all the stops made by Nos. 1 and 21, as well as calling at DeSoto, Arcadia-Ironton, and Piedmont, Missouri, and Prescott, Arkansas.

At Little Rock, Pullman cars originating in Memphis were added to the consists of the mainline trains. No. 1, the west Texas section, picked up a Pullman bound for El Paso. No. 21, the San Antonio-Mexico City section, picked up a Memphis-Corpus Christi sleeper. This car was dropped at Palestine, Texas, where it was picked up by No. 31, the Gulf Coast section.

Further down the line, No. 21 dropped a St. Louis-Shreveport 12-1 Pullman at Gurdon, and a St. Louis-El Dorado 12-1 car at Hope, Arkansas. No. 31 picked up no cars at Little Rock, but did drop a Lake Charles 10-1-2 Pullman that would be forwarded by Train 101, the Little Rock-Lake Charles *Louisiana Sunshine Special*. Companion Train 102 returned the car to Little Rock at 11:15pm, in time to be picked up by No. 22 for the remainder of the run to St. Louis.

Because of the *Sunshine's* national reputation, and because virtually all its end-points were warm-weather destinations, the trains were a magnet for through cars from other railroads. Beginning in 1946, through car service was inaugurated between New York-Washington and the southwest over the New York Central, Baltimore and Ohio, and the Pennsylvania Railroad.

This added further complexity to an already busy operation, and made strict adherence to the timetable even more critical if connections were to be maintained at MoPac's "St. Louis Gateway."

In May, 1948, the roster of through sleepers handled by the *Sunshine Specials* included:

The first public notice of the impending arrival of the *Texas Eagles* came in 1946, when MoPac proudly announced a $12 million order for new streamlined passenger cars:

"With the inauguration of new equipment, the *Sunshine Special* will become the *Sunshine Eagle*. Eastern lines that now operate through sleeping cars via the *Sunshine* have also ordered new streamlined cars to match those being built for the *Sunshine Eagle*.

"Two of the four new *Eagle* trains will operate between St. Louis and Dallas-Fort Worth-El Paso and two between St. Louis and Houston-Galveston-San Antonio and Mexico City, the latter service in connection with the National Lines of Mexico."

As it developed, MoPac's plan to name their new Texas trains the *Sunshine Eagle* would go unfulfilled, as the N de M never got around to acquiring streamlined sleepers for the through-car pool. For this reason, the MoPac trains were rechristened *Texas Eagles* and operated only as far as San Antonio. The new equipment began arriving in 1948, and was introduced into immediate service on the *Sunshine Special*. Enthused the railroad in its Summer timetable:

"Many Missouri Pacific patrons have already enjoyed a sample of *Texas Eagle* service. Streamlined coaches and all-room sleeping cars have been operating in the *Sunshine Special* for several weeks and other new cars will be added as rapidly as they are delivered. For Missouri Pacific has chosen not to wait until the *Texas Eagles* are complete trains-it prefers to provide its best ser-

Train(s)	Car Type	Between	Forwarded by
1	14-4	New York-Fort Worth	New York Central
1	8-1-2	Washington-Fort Worth	Baltimore & Ohio
1-2	10-1-2	St. Louis-Los Angeles	Southern Pacific
1-2	14-4	New York-El Paso	Pennsylvania
1-2	1 DR/3DBR/Lounge	New York-Fort Worth	Pennsylvania
2	8-1-2	Fort Worth-New York	New York Central
2	8-1-2	Fort Worth-New York	Baltimore & Ohio
21	12-1	St. Louis-Shreveport	Louisiana & Arkansas (KCS)
21-22	10-1-2	St. Louis-Mexico City	N. de M.
21-22	12-1	St. Louis-Mexico City	N. de M.
21-22	14-4	New York-San Antonio	Pennsylvania
21-22	10-1-2	Washington-San Antonio	Chesapeake & Ohio/NYC
22	12-1	Shreveport-St. Louis	Kansas City Southern
31-32	10-5	New York-Houston	Pennsylvania
31-32	10-1-2	Washington-Galveston	Pennsylvania
31-32	8-5	New York-Houston	New York Central

Below: One of those E6 sets purchased for the *Colorado Eagle* has strayed far from home as it heads Train 7, the southbound *Southerner* at Texarkana in September, 1950. More than a full decade into the *Eagle* era, the consist is a mixed bag of blue and green heavyweight equipment. *Joe Collias*

vice as soon as possible. That policy, too, is part of the Missouri Pacific tradition of travel leadership throughout the West and Southwest."

The order for new *Texas Eagle* equipment consisted of 69 coaches, food service and head-end cars from ACF, and another 47 sleepers from Pullman-Standard for service on the joint MP-T&P service. According to the railroad, the new cars were as fine as anything on wheels:

"The passenger carrying equipment of the *Eagle* trains includes several types of cars not heretofore used by the Missouri Pacific. Dormitory-coaches have seats for 52 passengers and sleeping accommodations for the dining car crew; other coaches seat 64 passen-

gers in divided sections, while still another kind are the deluxe coaches seating 60.

"All coaches feature roomy, deeply up-holstered seats, fully reclining under finger-tip control, and with adjustable footrests. Reading lights over each pair of seats are recessed into the underside of the fully enclosed luggage rack. The cars are decorated

Right: With the exception of MoPac's in-bound commuter job, trains entering St. Louis Union Station first pulled past the trainshed, then backed in. Here, the "deuces" are wild as *Texas Eagle* No. 2 and *Texas Special* No. 2 arrive in St. Louis simultaneously (don't be fooled by the *Colorado Eagle* logo on the nose of E6 - No. 12 didn't arrive until after noon). The *Broadway* and the *Century* had nothing on these two competitors! *Louis Marre collection*

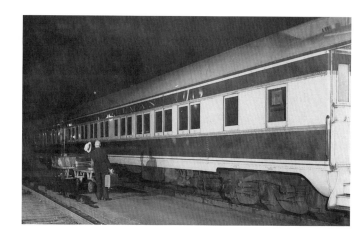

Above: The first day of *Texas Eagle* operation is only one day away as T&P 14-1-2 sleeper *Eagle Flight* poses for a birthday picture outside the Pullman-Standard plant on August 14, 1948. *Eagle Flight* was converted to coach 405 at Sedalia in 1964. *Alan Wayne Hegler collection*

Below: Backbone of the MP-T&P Pullman fleet were the 38 14-4 sleepers outshopped by Pullman-Standard in 1948. *Eagle Hill* served on the MoPac for 21 years before being sold to the FCP (Pacific Railroad) of Mexico in 1969, where she was rechristened *Rio Alamos*. *Charlie Duckworth collection*

Bottom: *Eagle Canyon* was one of three 5 double bedroom, 27 seat "soda fountain" lounge cars. Originally conceptualized as observation cars, they were finally built with blind ends having inset, backlit transparencies simulating windows. *Eagle Ridge* was converted to RPO 387 in 1966. *Eagle Cliff* survives today in private ownership, still painted in *Eagle colors*. *Alan Wayne Hegler collection*

Above: Primarily used by employees of Lion Oil Company, 10-1-2 sleepers *Paris Gibson* and twin *Marcus Daly* worked the *Sunshine Special* between St. Louis and El Dorado, Arkansas. Here, *Paris Gibson* loads passengers at St. Louis Union Station in the late 1940's. Note the block of air conditioning ice on the first baggage cart. *Charlie Duckworth collection*

Below: In the early 1960's, 12-1 Pullman *Armington* was repainted into the red and cream colors of the N de M and assigned to *Aztec Eagle* service between San Antonio and Mexico City. Before heading south of the border, however, the car worked Gulf Coast Lines-SAU&G Trains 215-216 between San Antonio and Mission, Texas. *R. H. Carlson photo, Charlie Duckworth collection*

Bottom: We're outside ACF's St. Charles, Missouri plant for a preview look at T&P diner-lounge 526. Along with sisters 525 and 527, the cars were built in 1948 for service on the new *Texas Eagles*. Cars 525 and 526 were sold in 1969. The 527 was scrapped in 1966. *Charlie Duckworth collection*

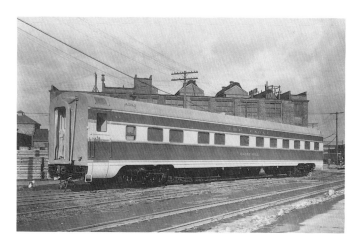

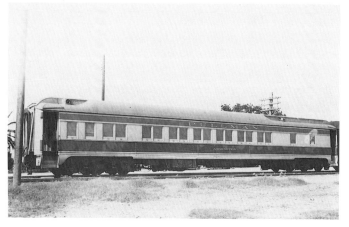

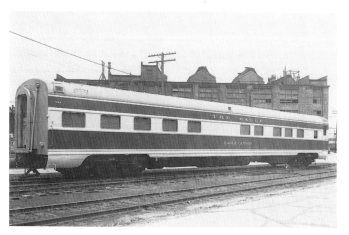

Above: Unlike parent Missouri Pacific, which had only one color for its steam power (black), in 1948 always-individualistic T&P painted several of its P-1 Pacifics in *Eagle* blue and gray. A few, including class engine 700 also got side skirting with the *Eagle* train name applied. The locomotives worked the road's *Louisiana Eagle* and *Louisiana Limited*. *C. R. Scholes photo, Kevin EuDaly collection*

Below: Dormitory-coaches 820-823 were delivered in 1948 and sublettered for MoPac (820-822) and subsidiary International-Great Northern (823). In addition to service on the "West" *Texas Eagles*, the cars occasionally worked the *Colorado Eagle* between Denver and St. Louis. *ACF photo, Alan Wayne Hegler collection*

tastefully in pastel colors and have deep-pile carpets on the floors. Radios in each car provide standard broadcast programs.

"The diner-lounge cars for the *Eagles* seat 32 in the dining room, while the lounge section seats another 18. The new dining cars, handling 44 persons at a time, employ a new design in seating arrangements, the unique 'serpentine' seats in the center section presenting an interesting new aspect of this car."

Appointments and color schemes were typical of the era. Coaches were decorated with yellow ceilings and luggage racks and tan walls. Bulkheads at the women's lounge end of the car were decorated with photomurals. Carpets were garnet and the linoleum in the lounges was deep red. Grill-coaches were divided by decorative aluminum grille work attached to a seat-high partition between the coach seats and the dinette area.

Following the introduction of the *Texas Eagle*, MoPac also updated its dining car service plate by issuing a new version with the *Texas Eagle* in the center surrounded by the state capitals through which the railroad operated.

Sleeping cars in the 1948 order included 38 14-4 cars and six unique-to-the-MoPac 14-2-1 cars. In addition, three 5 double bedroom-26 seat "soda fountain" lounge-sleepers originally designed (but not built) as blunt-end observation

cars were acquired for use on the St. Louis-El Paso run. Likely because of the complicated set-out switching operations that took place during the trains' runs, observation cars were never included in the consists of any of the *Texas Eagles.*

In addition to the MoPac equipment, several 10-5 sleepers furnished by the Pennsylvania and the Baltimore & Ohio railroads and painted in *Eagle* blue and gray livery operated between New York, Washington, and Texas in the consists of the *Texas Eagles.* Finally, in 1952, five Pullman-Standard domes were purchased for the Fort Worth and San Antonio trains.

Following their August introduction, the new *Eagles* operated in two sections. Though not formally identified as such in public timetables, Trains 1 and 2 became known as the "West" *Texas Eagle*, and operated between St. Louis-Memphis and Dallas, Fort Worth and El Paso. In a break with practice established by the *Sunshine*, through car service to Los Angeles was no longer offered. Instead, California connections were made with the Southern Pacific at El Paso via Train No. 7, the *Southerner.*

Texas Eagles 21-22 were known as the "South" *Texas Eagles*, and ran between St. Louis-Memphis and Houston, Galveston, Austin, and San Antonio. These trains provided connections with the *Aztec Eagle* between San Antonio and Mexico City. Cross-border connections with the N de M were made at Laredo, Texas.

To illustrate how the operation worked, the May, 1950 timetable showed both the south and west Texas sections leaving St. Louis at 5:30pm. Departing from prior *Sunshine* practice, however, No. 21 rather than No. 1 was the lead section. The two sections carded stops at Little Rock at 12:10 and 12:20am to pick up their respective through cars from No. 201, the Memphis section.

The next stops for the *Eagles* were at Texarkana, Marshall, and Longview, Texas, where the old I-GN and T&P routes diverged. From

Longview, No. 1 turned west over the T&P for Dallas and Fort Worth before arriving in El Paso at 10:00pm Mountain Time, twenty-nine and a half hours after departing St. Louis.

No. 21, meanwhile, headed south over the I-GN for Austin and San Antonio. At Palestine, the south Texas and Gulf Coast sections split, with the latter arriving in Houston at 10:00am and Galveston at 11:55am. The south Texas section, meanwhile, arrived in San Antonio at 11:40am. Twenty-five minutes later, at 12:05pm, the *Aztec Eagle*, also operating as No. 21, departed for the run to Laredo, Monterrey, and Mexico City, where it arrived at 8:30pm the second day out.

With the *Texas Eagles* in daily service, the *Sunshine Special* was cut back to a single section. The abbreviated operation ran as Trains 31-32, with daily service between St. Louis-Memphis and El Dorado, Arkansas, Shreveport, and Lake Charles, Louisiana, and Austin and San Antonio, Texas.

Unlike the *Eagles*, which were regularly assigned streamlined equipment only, the *Sunshine* still operated with heavyweight cars. These included an 8-1-2 El Dorado sleeper, an 8-5 Lake Charles car, a 12-1 Pullman for San Antonio, and a northbound 10-1-2 Little Rock set-out sleeper.

Scheduled departure time from St. Louis for No. 31 was 5:35pm. Arrival at Little Rock was at 1:05am, where the sleepers for Hot Springs and Lake Charles were dropped off. Following a 1:35am departure, the *Sunshine* dropped the El Dorado sleeper at Gurdon and the Shreveport sleeper at Hope, Arkansas. South of Texarkana, No. 31 assumed chores of a local nature, making positive stops at 16 stations before its eventual 3:45pm arrival in San Antonio.

Northbound, *Texas Eagle* No. 2 departed El Paso at 12:30am, arriving Dallas at 6:00pm and St. Louis at 8:10 the following morning. Enroute, No. 2 dropped its Memphis cars at Little Rock following a 1:10am arrival; switch-

ers had to move briskly, as the schedule allowed only a 20-minute layover before departure at 1:30am.

No. 22, the *Aztec Eagle*, departed Mexico City at 8:00am with a 1:30pm arrival in San Antonio the following afternoon. *Texas Eagle* No. 22 departed San Antonio at 2:10pm and arrived at St. Louis at 8:20 the next morning. Enroute, No. 22 picked up the Houston section at Palestine at 6:55pm and dropped its Memphis cars at Little Rock at 1:20am. Departure for St. Louis was at 1:40am. Memphis connection No. 202 followed No. 22 out of town at 2:30am for a leisurely four-hour jaunt over its 149-mile route.

Meanwhile, *Sunshine* No. 32 departed San Antonio at 8:15am and arrived in St. Louis the following morning at 7:50. Enroute, it picked up a Shreveport sleeper bound for St. Louis at Texarkana, an El Dorado-St. Louis sleeper at Gurdon, and sleepers from Hot Springs and Lake Charles plus a set-out car at Little Rock.

Like most long-haul passenger trains of the era, the *Texas Eagles* underwent a number of revisions in their equipment and schedules. During the early years of operation, however, these changes were minor and had little effect on the trains' appearance or operation.

In 1951, for example, a Dallas-Los Angeles Pullman was added to the consist of No. 1. Although the June 17 timetable does not specify ownership, this was likely a Southern Pacific car. In addition, the 10-5 sleeper formerly assigned between Washington and Houston now was shown as a 10-6 car, and the 10-6 sleeper between New York and San Antonio was replaced by a 10-5.

Running times for the southbound *Eagles* were unaffected, although No. 31's schedule was lengthened by 10 minutes between Palestine and San Antonio. Arrival was now at 3:55pm. Northbound, No. 2 departed El Paso at 12:50 instead of 12:30am. Arrival times in St. Louis for Trains 2, 22, and 32 were not changed.

In 1952 the big news was the addition of Planetarium dome cars to Nos. 21-22 on July 1, and Nos. 1-2 on July 12. Dome cars operated

between St. Louis and Fort Worth and St. Louis and San Antonio.

No. 1's schedule was extended 15 minutes between Fort Worth and El Paso, pushing arrival back to 10:15pm. No. 31 was slowed by 30 minutes between Palestine and San Antonio, delaying arrival until 4:25pm. Local trains 231-232 between Memphis and Newport, Arkansas were discontinued, effective January 2.

Perhaps reflecting the changing social climate, "divided" (Jim Crow) coaches, though still in operation, were no longer identified in 1953 timetable equipment listings. Also in that year, the Texarkana-San Antonio cafe-parlor car carried in the consist of No. 31 was dropped in favor of a buffet-coach between Marshall and Fort Worth.

Departure time for Nos. 1 and 21 was pushed back to 5:45pm. Arrival in El Paso for No. 1 was changed to 10:30pm, and arrival time in San Antonio was now 12:20pm for No. 21. At the same time, the 14-4 sleeper from St. Louis was extended to Laredo instead of terminating in San Antonio. The San Antonio-Mexico City dining car, however, was dropped, and the 8-5 Mexico City Pullman was replaced by an 8-3-1 car.

Departure from St. Louis for No. 31 was advanced to 5:15pm, and the operation was rerouted from San Antonio to Fort Worth, with an arrival time of 10:45am. The northbound

Above: PA-1 8003 seems impatient to be underway at it leads *Texas Eagle* No. 22 north out of Austin, Texas in the summer of 1951. At Palestine, No. 22 will meet the Houston section, No. 26-22, where the two will combine for the overnight run to St. Louis. Included in the consist is a San Antonio-New York Pullman that will continue east from St. Louis via the PRR. *Photo by R. S. Plummer, Joe Collias collection*

Below: Trains 131-132 were known as the *Louisiana Sunshine Specials* and handled coaches, a grill coach and an 8-5 sleeper between Lake Charles and Little Rock, where the Pullman was handed off to No. 31-32 for St. Louis. Here, No. 132 rips through Tioga, Louisiana on July 13, 1952. *A. E. Brown photo, Charlie Duckworth collection*

Big Red

For nearly half a century, Missouri Pacific's principal competition between St. Louis and the Southwest was the joint Frisco-Katy *Texas Special*. The *Texas Special* was originally introduced on December 15, 1915 (the same year Iron Mountain inaugurated its premier *Sunshine Special*) as a Missouri-Kansas-Texas train operating between St. Louis, Kansas City and San Antonio, Texas.

The *Special's* career as a Katy-only train was short-lived, however. At the beginning of the United States' entry into World War I, at direction of the USRA, M-K-T entered into an agreement with the St. Louis-San Francisco Railway in March, 1917 to jointly operate the train over the 1,039 mile run between St. Louis and San Antonio.

As a result of the agreement, Frisco's *Meteor* was cut back from Texas to the St. Louis-Oklahoma City train it remained until it was discontinued in 1965.

The route of the *Texas Special* was St. Louis to Vinita, Oklahoma via the Frisco, and then over the M-K-T to Dallas-Fort Worth and San Antonio. Equipment included deluxe coaches, dining car and Pullman service, and a buffet-observation-lounge car, including lounge *William B. Travis*, that was the last heavyweight lounge car built (in 1937) in the United States.

Power for the heavyweight version of the *Special* was typically one of Frisco's 1500-series 4-8-2's north of Vinita and a Katy 400-series Pacific over the Oklahoma and Texas flatlands.

The Pacifics hung on for a year or so after dieselization owing to the train's short turn-around time in San Antonio. Until additional diesels arrived on the Katy, steam continued to handle the train between Waco and San Antonio. This permitted Katy shop crews additional time to service the new, initially unfamiliar, motive power.

The timetable called for an early evening departure from St. Louis, with arrival in San Antonio the following evening. Northbound, departure was at 8:00am, with arrival in St. Louis at 8:30 the next morning.

With the coming of diesel power, running times were shortened somewhat. Frisco's October, 1956 timetable called for southbound times of 5:40pm-2:59pm and 11:40am-8:00am on the return. These times were very similar to the running times for MoPac's *Texas Eagles*.

The *Texas Special* operated as a heavyweight train until 1948, when streamlined equipment built by Pullman-Standard began to arrive on the Frisco and the Katy. The order included 28 cars for the *Special*: Two RPO-baggage cars, six coaches, two coach-buffet-lounges, two full

Below: In this early photo of Frisco-Katy's *Texas Special*, southbound No. 1 poses at Dallas in 1949 with the original streamlined consist, including the RPO, coach, coach-buffet-lounge, chair, diner and six Pullman sleepers, including a round-end observation. *R. S. Plummer photo, Raymond George collection*

Above: In this later view of the *Texas Special*, northbound No. 2 rolls through Bruceville, Texas in 1952. By this time, the star had been removed from the locomotives' noses and replaced by a Katy herald. Nine cars were the normal consist between San Antonio and Dallas, but today it looks as though several extra heavyweight cars have been added. *R. S. Plummer photo, Raymond George collection*

dining cars, fourteen 14-4 sleepers and a pair of 2 bedroom-1 drawing room observation lounge cars. In addition, four EMD E7 locomotives were ordered in 1947 as power for the re-equipped train.

Ownership of the *Texas Special* equipment, including the locomotives, was evenly divided between Frisco and M-K-T. The trains operated as identical 14-car consists.

The *Specials* were painted a stunning combination of bright red window panels and roofs and maroon skirting. Letterboards and side panels were fluted, stainless steel. The locomotives were painted red with yellow and silver trim and stainless side panels. All the cars were named for on-line cities and famous individuals from Missouri and Texas history, including *David Crockett, Sam Houston, Stephen Austin* and *Joseph Pulitzer*.

For a season, the *Texas Special* was a highly successful train, with a cachet more than equal to that of MoPac's *Sunshine* and *Texas Eagle*. Following the end of the Korean War, however, the Katy entered a period of serious economic decline that led, in 1957, to the appointment of William N. Deramus III as the company's president.

Deramus immediately embarked on a program of cost-cutting that quickly led to a reduction in both the quantity and quality of the road's passenger operations. Maintenance of both rolling stock and the physical plant suffered, causing frequent delays of up to 14 hours.

At the same time, Katy obtained a mail contract for the train that provided additional revenue, but caused timekeeping to deteriorate even further. Frisco quickly lost patience with the bad maintenance and sloppy timekeeping, and in January, 1959, dropped its end of the operation. The streamlined equipment was shifted to Frisco's other feature train, the *Kansas City-Florida Special*.

The *Texas Special* soldiered on for a few more years in increasingly dog-eared condition as a Katy-only Kansas City-San Antonio operation. By the time John Barriger arrived on the scene in 1964 at the head of still another new management team, the *Special* and the railroad itself were nearly beyond saving. In an effort to conserve cash, the *Texas Special* and its companion day trains, the *Katy Flyers*, were discontinued on June 30, 1965.

The name was revived one last time nearly twenty years later in the 1980's, when the MKT ran a pair hot piggyback trains between Kansas City and Dallas named appropriately enough, the *Texas Special*.

schedule for No. 2 was unchanged. No. 22 was combined with No. 26 between Laredo and San Antonio. Departure was at 9:05am from Laredo and 2:10pm from San Antonio, with arrival in St. Louis for No. 22 at 8:20am.

Northbound No. 32 was cut back to Texarkana-St. Louis only. Departure time was 7:45pm with arrival in St. Louis at 7:30am. The St. Louis-San Antonio Pullman handled by Southerner No. 7 made its last run on March 6.

In 1954, the St. Louis-Galveston sleeper on Trains 21-22 was cut back to Houston on January 10, ending through car service to that city. Departure time for Nos. 1 and 21 from St. Louis returned to 5:30pm. Arrival times in El Paso and Laredo were unchanged, however, in effect lengthening the previous schedule by 15 minutes.

The St. Louis-Laredo sleeper inaugurated the previous August was dropped on March 14, and in April, the 10-1-2 San Antonio Pullman was upgraded to a streamlined 14-4. Southbound *Sunshine* No. 31 was cut back from St. Louis-Fort Worth to St. Louis-Texarkana, an indication that time had begun running out for this historic operation.

No equipment or schedule changes appeared in the April 24, 1955 timetable. An advertisement on page 7, however, did note that the Missouri Pacific Railroad was now "100% Dieselized." Also of interest was a "public service" advertisement appealing for a greater share of US Mail traffic, citing higher rates (read subsidies) paid to airlines and trucking companies.

The December 18, 1955 timetable showed the following changes: The St. Louis-Fort Worth sleeper carried in the consist of No. 1 was extended to Chicago via GM&O's *Limited* southbound and *Abraham Lincoln* northbound. The St. Louis-Houston sleeper was also extended to Chicago.

The Shreveport, El Dorado, Hot Springs, and Lake Charles sleepers carried in the consist of Train 31 were switched to *Texas Eagle* No. 1. Train 31 was then discontinued as a separate schedule between St. Louis and Little Rock and operated as a coach-only local between Little Rock and Texarkana. Northbound, the *Sunshine* continued to operate as a full consist between Texarkana and St. Louis, departing at 7:45pm and arriving at 7:50am.

Departure from St. Louis remained 5:30pm for No. 21, but delayed until 5:45pm for No. 1,

to ensure the connection with GM&O No. 1. Arrival in El Paso for *Texas Eagle* No. 1 now was 10:45pm, 15 minutes later than previously. Running time for No. 21 was shortened 10 minutes end-to-end, with several changes between intermediate points along the way. Northbound, No. 2's schedule was unchanged. No. 22's schedule was extended 5 minutes, with arrival in St. Louis at 8:25am. The Memphis section, still scheduled for 4 hours from Little Rock, now departed at 3:30am instead of 2:30.

In 1956, the last new streamlined passenger-carrying equipment purchased by the MoPac, six Budd 10-6 sleepers were placed in service in the consists of *Eagles* 21-22 between Chicago and Houston and *Southerners* 7-8 between Chicago and Hot Springs.

Perhaps in deference to the light rail in use on the Hot Springs branch, the cars were built with six-wheeled trucks, unusual for streamlined, lightweight equipment. Both cars were

forwarded by the GM&O between Chicago and St. Louis. In August, the St. Louis-San Antonio through coach handled by Trains 7-8 was discontinued.

The Chicago-Houston sleeper carried in the consist of Nos. 1 and 2 between St. Louis and Texarkana was switched in 1957 to Nos. 21 and 22 over their entire MoPac routing. The St. Louis-Hot Springs Budd sleeper formerly in the consist of No. 7 was switched to No. 1 between St. Louis and Little Rock. A diner-lounge was added to Nos. 1 and 2 between Fort Worth and El Paso; previously, no dining service had been available on this portion of the route.

No changes were made to the consists of Nos. 21 or 22 except for the Chicago sleeper noted above. Departure from St. Louis was now 5:40pm for No. 21 and 5:50pm for No. 1. Arrival times in Houston, Laredo and El Paso remained unchanged, in effect speeding up end-to-end times by a few minutes. Arrival and

Right: Trains 219-220 were Hot Springs-Memphis runs that forwarded a coach and a 10-6 sleeper between Hot Springs and Little Rock, where they were picked up by No. 8 for the rest of the run to St. Louis. On June 15, 1960, No. 220 heads out of Little Rock for Bald Knob, Arkansas, where it will turn east for a 7:00pm arrival in Memphis. *J. Parker Lamb*

departure times for all northbound sections remained the same.

The *Texas Eagles'* tenth anniversary year was comparatively uneventful, with no timetable revisions and only nominal changes to train consists.

In January, 1958, the New York-El Paso Pullman interchanged with Pennsylvania's *Penn-Texas* by *Eagle* No. 1 was cut back to New York-Fort Worth. The service was replaced by a Chicago-El Paso car which formerly terminated in Fort Worth. This car was picked up in St. Louis by No. 21 and was handed off to No. 1 in Little Rock. The return routing to Chicago was via MoPac Trains 22 and 2, and GM&O's *Abraham Lincoln*.

On the south Texas runs, a grill coach was added to the consists of Trains 21 and 22 between St. Louis and San Antonio, furnishing an economical alternative meal service in addition to the diner-lounge. On May 1, Missouri Pacific's low-priced "Travel Tray" meal service was instituted on all *Eagle* trains. Sixty days later, Train No. 4 was discontinued south of Little Rock, and in September, through car service between St. Louis and Corpus Christi was dropped.

In 1959, No. 31, the coach-only *Sunshine Special* remnant between Little Rock and Texarkana was dropped from the timetable. The El Dorado and Shreveport sleepers formerly set out

Above: The name *Texas Eagle* conjures up an image of 14-car streamliners streaking between St. Louis and Texas, but in fact, that was only the case as far south as Longview and Palestine. After that, the *Eagles* fragmented into a series of local trains serving widely separated end points. In January, 1953, car tonks wipe down the windows of 14-1-2 sleeper *Eagle County* during No. 122-22's short layover at Galveston, Texas. *Charlie Duckworth collection*

Below: Missouri Pacific purchased no "PB" units to go with its 36-unit fleet of Alco PA passenger units, so when extra power was called for, E7B's were often asked to stand in. On a mild January 18, 1958, PA-1 8010 leads the *Texan* across Iron Street in St. Louis. *Jim Ozment photo, Charlie Duckworth collection*

Above: Texas & Pacific F7's 1500, 1501, 1581 and 1582 along with F7B's 1531-1534 were painted for passenger service to assist the E-units when a full 4,000 horsepower was not needed. The F-units, however, did not have steam boilers. *E. M. Kahn photo, Louis Marre collection*

by No. 1 at Little Rock now continued in the consist of that train to Gurdon and Hope, Arkansas. Ironically, with this change, No. 1 was beginning to look and operate in a manner not unlike the old *Sunshine* when it ran with a full consist from St. Louis.

Further south, the grill-coach operating between San Antonio and Laredo on the *Aztec Eagle* was dropped southbound, but added northbound. In June, the 10-6 sleeper between Washington and Houston was removed from the consist of No. 21. Also discontinued was the second 14-4 Pullman between San Antonio and St. Louis.

In October, MoPac leased a Budd-built 24 roomette, 8 double bedroom Slumbercoach. Primarily intended to serve the military trade, the car operated between Baltimore and San Antonio via B&O's *National Limited* and MoPac 21-22.

The Dallas-El Paso Pullman was dropped from the consist of Train 7, the *Southerner*, ending sleeper service in west Texas on that train. The Chicago-Hot Springs Pullman handled in the consists of Memphis-Hot Springs Trains 219-220 were reassigned to Little Rock-Hot Springs locals 831-832. Finally, Train 26 between Palestine and Little Rock was cut back to Texarkana and combined with Train 4 to St. Louis.

Below: In the early 1960's, MoPac undertook the repainting of all its motive power and passenger equipment, with the result that the Loewy-designed *Eagle* blue and gray quickly disappeared under a coat of solid "Jenks" blue. In this June 13, 1962 photo, taken at Texarkana, can be seen the "before and after" of the repainting program. *Steve Patterson*

Right: Texas & Pacific Trains 26-27, the *Louisiana Daylights* ran between New Orleans and Marshall, Texas, where they connected with MoPac 7-8, the *Southerners* on the run to San Antonio. Here, T&P E8 2015 leads a spic-and-span consist near Shreveport, Louisiana on a winter afternoon in 1955. *A. E. Brown photo, Louis Marre collection*

Changes during the year 1960 were relatively minimal. The 8-5 Pullman handled in the consist of *Aztec Eagles* 21-22 was upgraded to an 8-1-3 car, and in December, to a streamlined 10-5 sleeper. The El Paso-Chicago Pullman formerly handed off by No. 2 to No. 22 at Little Rock now rode all the way to St. Louis in the consist of No. 2. Memphis-Hot Springs Train 219 began forwarding a St. Louis through coach handled by No. 7 between St. Louis and Little Rock. No. 25, the southbound *Texan*, added a through St. Louis-Fort Worth coach.

Northbound *Southerner* No. 8 added several through cars to its consist, including a grill-coach from Ft. Worth to Marshall, a diner lounge between Texarkana and St. Louis, a Hot Springs-St. Louis through coach picked up in Little Rock, and a Fort Worth-Memphis coach that was handed off to Train 220 at Little Rock. No changes in end-point arrival or departure times were made.

If one year could be singled out as the beginning of retrenchment for Missouri Pacific's Texas service, it would be 1961. The biggest change took place on September 24, when the South and West *Texas Eagles* were combined between St. Louis and Texarkana. Operating as Train No. 1-21-121 and 122-22-2, the consolidated *Texas Eagle* departed St. Louis at 5:30pm. Arrival in Texarkana was at 3:20am.

Train No. 1, the west Texas section, departed Texarkana at 3:40am, followed by the combined south Texas sections at 3:45am. Arrival times for No. 1 in Dallas was at 8:10am and in El Paso at 10:45pm. The south Texas section, meanwhile, operated as a single train between Texarkana and Palestine. There, No. 21 headed for San Antonio and Laredo while No. 121 turned south for Houston. Arrival times for the trains were at 11:40am in Houston and 1:30pm in San Antonio.

Right: Three Alco PA's smoke it up on the lead of No. 8, the northbound *Southerner* **as it crosses the Arkansas River at Little Rock in June, 1960. Look quickly at these brutes, for they will be off the roster by 1964.** *J. Parker Lamb photo, Louis Marre collection*

Because of the length of the combined *Eagle*, the usual procedure was to employ three adjacent tracks at St. Louis to assemble the trains. According to an internal memo dated April 1, the train would be staged on Tracks 4, 5 and 6 as follows:

TRACK 6

Car Type	Operating between
RPO	St. Louis-Houston
RPO-Storage Mail	St. Louis-Dallas
Storage Mail-Dorm	St. Louis-Fort Worth
Coach-Dormitory	St. Louis-Houston
Coach	St. Louis-Houston

TRACK 5

Car Type	Operating between
Sleeper	Chicago-Houston
Sleeper	New York-Houston
Sleeper	New York-San Antonio
Slumbercoach	Baltimore-San Antonio
Diner-Lounge	St. Louis-San Antonio
Dome Coach	St. Louis-San Antonio
Grill Coach	St. Louis-San Antonio
Sleeper	St. Louis-San Antonio
Coach	St. Louis-El Paso
Dome Coach	St. Louis-Fort Worth
Coach	St. Louis-Forth Worth
Dining Car	St. Louis-Fort Worth
Sleeper	St. Louis-Fort Worth

TRACK 4

Car Type	Operating between
Sleeper	Chicago-Fort Worth
Sleeper	New York-Fort Worth
Sleeper	Baltimore-Fort Worth
Sleeper	St. Louis-Lake Charles

Moving the train out of the station was a complicated process:

"After the passing (through) sleepers are positioned on Tracks 4 and 5, it will be necessary to double Track 5 to Track 4. Track 6 will not be doubled until after the three RPO and storage-mail cars have been loaded and released by postal authorities due to the fact that Track 18, the longest track in St. Louis Union Station will hold only 18 cars with part of the 18th car off the platform."

It was planned that the combined train would leave St. Louis with 22 cars in the consist, not including "any additional cars which are normally handled during the summer months and holiday seasons."

As it developed, the *Texas Eagle* still occasionally operated in multiple sections, most often during the heavy summer and Christmas travel periods. The last time the *Eagle* ran in three sections was on a bitterly cold December 22, 1961, when separate Fort Worth, Houston and San Antonio sections moved more than 50 cars and 1,500 people out of St. Louis. Demand for space was so heavy that heavyweight sleepers and even a 5 double bedroom sleeper-lounge car were pressed into coach service. Many riders sat up all night, but nobody had to stand.

There were other service reductions as well. Through sleeping car service to Memphis was reduced to a single Fort Worth Pullman, as the Houston car was discontinued on April 15. Train 32, the Texarkana-St. Louis remnant of the old *Sunshine Special* was downgraded to a coach-only operation over the entire route.

Head-end heavy Trains 7-8 continued to offer coach, grill-coach and 6-6-4 sleeping car service between El Paso and Dallas, as well as a southbound 10-5 car between St. Louis and Hot Springs. Northbound, the Hot Springs car was handled in the consist of No. 2-22 between Little Rock and St. Louis.

Another cutback not directly related to train operations was the elimination of the traditional four-color public timetable that had been a MoPac staple since the mid-1940's. In its place was a drab, duotone folder that featured a stylized passenger train pulled by Alco PA 8002 painted in traditional *Eagle* colors.

By the following year, even this would be downgraded, as the train was depicted in Jenks blue. The PA would be renumbered 25, in keeping with the general equipment renumbering that took place in the early 1960's.

For reasons unrelated to the economics of running the railroad, 1962 began badly for the *Texas Eagle*. On the night of January 16, 20-car No. 1 collided with an overturned hopper car just north of DeSoto, Missouri. The offending hopper was one of five cars that were shoved off the end of a stub siding paralleling the mail line. Apparently, the flagman working the switch job

Below: T&P Train 25, the *Louisiana Daylight* departs New Orleans Union Passenger Terminal on April 20, 1963. In the consist of the head-end heavy *Daylight* are express cars, coaches and a grill coach that will run as far as Marshall, Texas. *J. W. Swanberg*

Above: Amply powered Train 22, the northbound *Texas Eagle*, rolls into Austin, Texas in the summer of 1964. Visible behind the RPO are Slumbercoach *Southland* and one of the Pullman-Standard Planetarium dome coaches. Also in the consist are a diner-lounge, a standard coach and sleeping cars from San Antonio and Mexico City. *J. Parker Lamb*

Right: Little Rock switcher 6012 waits for *Southerner* No. 7 to come to a stop so it can begin shuffling head end cars in and out of the consist. Note the mixed bag of power on this August morning in 1963. No. 7 has consumed nearly 10 hours on her 349-mile overnight run from St. Louis. *Steve Patterson*

lost count of the number of cars already in the siding, and tried to add more cars than the capacity of the track. Five cars were shoved off the rails. Four went down the bank of nearby Joachim Creek. The fifth fell directly across the main track. What happened next was described by engineer William Wagner:

"I'm getting to be an old man (65), and sometimes old men see things that aren't there. So when we approached Mooney's Bridge, I hesitated a split second because I couldn't believe what I saw. But it was real-an overturned black hopper car fouling the main track on the fireman's side.

"Well, I big-holed 'er, but at 55 MPH that isn't going to do much in a few hundred feet. I told the fireman to move over to my side of the cab and stand behind me, since the car was

Left: In the twilight of her career, PA-3 77 leads a pair of passenger GP7's on *Texas Eagle* No. 1 out of Austin in June, 1964. Before the end of the year, MoPac's Alco fleet will be retired in favor of E's and steam generator-equipped Geeps. *J. Parker Lamb*

Below: As older E6 and E7 units began to disappear from the passenger roster, steam boiler-equipped GP7's began showing up on more and more schedules. In this May 22, 1965 photo, Geep 313 powers the *Texas Eagle* at Dallas, Texas. *Joe McMillan*

Above: The mail clerk in the RPO prepares to hook a pouch of mail as *Texas Eagle* No. 2 blasts by a local freight at McNeil, Texas in June, 1965. E7 22 was acquired as International-Great Northern 7013 back in 1947. She's rolled up some miles in the last 18 years.
J. Parker Lamb

on his side. I've worked for the railroad all my life. I figured this was the way it was going to end, but what the hell - it's been a good life.

"We hit hard, and the windshield on my side shattered-disappeared into thin air. All I heard was ripping metal. The engine tottered, then rolled over to the right and down the embankment. As it slid forward, the empty cab window scooped up dirt and buried my legs. But my glasses didn't even break. And I had a clear block!"

Within a few days, Engineer Wagner was again working his regular runs.

The consequence of the derailment was three locomotives (PA 8035, E7B 7017B and PA 8018) went down the Joachim Creek embankment along with four head-end cars and the first coach. Nine more passenger cars were

derailed but upright on the right of way. The last six cars remained on the tracks.

The accident occurred at 7:03pm. By 8:45pm the St. Louis wrecker had been called out and was enroute. At 10:00 Alco PA 8008 was sent out light from St. Louis to pick up the six cars not derailed. The cars were returned to St. Louis at 1:31am. Passengers were removed from the wreck site with the assistance of 40 Air Force recruits in route to San Antonio.

Of the 284 aboard the *Eagle*, 82 would claim and eventually be compensated for injuries, including an English Lord. Back in St. Louis, a replacement train consisting of four coaches, seven Pullmans, and a diner was assembled and dispatched via Chester, Illinois, at 3:26am.

The main line was cleared by 6:25pm the following evening. The three locomotives and five cars that had gone down the embankment were frozen to the ground and were removed over the next several days.

On a less cataclysmic note, 1962 also saw a complete renumbering of Missouri Pacific passenger trains system-wide. The *Texas Eagles* now operated as Trains 1-21-41 southbound, and 42-22-2 northbound. Under the revised operating scheme, Trains 1-2 and 21-22 ex-

changed routes, as Nos. 21-22 became the west Texas section and Nos. 1-2 took over the run to San Antonio.

Concurrent with the revised assignments of the mainline trains, the *Aztec Eagle* also changed timetable numbers to Trains 1-2. Trains 121-122, the Houston section, were renumbered to 41-42.

Beginning in 1962, MoPac and Texas and Pacific timetables were combined, leading to the appearance of several T&P trains in the formerly MoPac-only publication. Foremost among these was the *Louisiana Eagle*, Trains 23-21 and 22-24, between New Orleans and El Paso.

Connections with the main stem of the *Texas Eagle* were made at Marshall, Texas. Through coaches and a 10-6 Pullman were operated between New Orleans and Fort Worth. A diner-lounge ran between New Orleans and Marshall.

Westbound, *Louisiana Eagle* No. 23 departed New Orleans at 8:00pm and arrived in Marshall at 4:40am. Departure for Fort Worth in the combined consist with No. 21 from St. Louis was at 5:25am. Eastbound, No. 22 arrived in Marshall at 9:05pm. Departure from Marshall was at 9:20pm, with arrival in New Orleans at 6:15 the next morning.

The other T&P trains appearing in the MoPac timetable were Nos. 25-27 and 28-26, the combined *Louisiana Daylight-Westerner*. The *Daylight-Westerners* were the daytime counterparts of the *Louisiana Eagle*. Like the *Eagles*, they operated between New Orleans and Marshall, where they met Nos. 7-27 and 28-8, the *Southerners*, on their runs between St. Louis and San Antonio-Houston-El Paso.

One *Texas Eagle* cutback that occurred in 1962 was the discontinuance of the Baltimore/ Washington-San Antonio Pullman operated in tandem with the B&O. This move left the Baltimore-San Antonio Slumbercoach as the last through car to run between St. Louis and the East. The Slumbercoach was withdrawn from service in May, 1964 and returned to Budd.

By the early 1960's, the *Southerner* had become something of a poor man's *Eagle*, with south and west Texas sections splitting at Texarkana. The south Texas section continued as Nos. 7-8 to San Antonio, while the west Texas section, called the *Westerner*, operated as Trains 27-28 to Dallas, Fort Worth and El Paso. Memphis-Hot Springs connecting Trains 37-38 joined the main stem at Little Rock. Coach-only Trains 47-48, the Houston section, split from the San Antonio train at Palestine. The Houston trains were discontinued on February 12, 1963.

No through cars from the T&P ran in either the San Antonio or the Houston sections of the

Above: An Illinois Central baggage car heads up the consist of No. 1 at Round Rock, Texas in February, 1966. According to the message board on the depot wall, the only trains scheduled to stop are Nos. 7-8, the *Southerners*. *J. Parker Lamb*

Texas Eagle. As a daytime operation that included no sleepers to or from New Orleans, *Texas Eagle* through cars handled by the *Daylight-Westerner* were limited to coaches between New Orleans-Fort Worth and New Orleans-El Paso. Daylight No. 25 departed New Orleans at 8:05am and arrived in Marshall at 4:25pm. On the return trip, No. 26 departed Marshall at 11:10am and arrived back in New Orleans at 8:35pm.

Southerner service underwent heavy downgrading beginning in 1964. On January 21, Memphis-Hot Springs connecting Trains 37-38 were discontinued between Little Rock and Hot Springs. Shortly after, MoPac abandoned the Hot Springs line and secured trackage rights over the parallel Rock Island. In February, the Memphis-Fort Worth through coach and the El Paso-Fort Worth diner were eliminated, and in April the Dallas-El Paso Pullman made its final run. In August, 1965, the Memphis-Little Rock connection was severed altogether, as 37-38 made their final runs. Main line Trains 7-8 were discontinued altogether on July 11, 1968. They were followed into history by coach-only St. Louis-Fort Worth Trains 3 and 4 on November 11, 1968.

Left: It's 1:45 in the afternoon as the inbound and outbound sections of the *Aztec Eagle* share the platform at San Antonio, Texas in August, 1964. The consist of the just-arrived *Texas Eagle* is visible behind the mail truck. By 2:15, No. 2 will be on its way back to St. Louis. *J. Parker Lamb*

As had been the case with the *Missouri River Eagle*, *Texas Eagle* cutbacks were fairly gradual. In March, 1963, the diner-coach operating between St. Louis and Houston was withdrawn in favor of a grill-coach, and the second, weekend-only sleeper was dropped.

In January, 1964, Little Rock-Lake Charles Trains 31-32 were cut back to Alexandria, Louisiana, and in November, 1967, discontinued altogether. Sadly, the Planetarium dome coaches were also withdrawn in 1967. All but one of the domes finished out their days on Illinois Central's *City of New Orleans* and *City of Miami*.

Despite the cutbacks, however, it was still possible in the summer of 1967 to board 14-4 and 10-6 sleeping cars in St. Louis for Fort Worth, Houston, San Antonio, Alexandria or Mexico City. In addition, through coaches continued to operate between New Orleans and Fort Worth on Trains 21-22 and 23-24, as did a 10-6 New Orleans-Fort Worth sleeper on Trains 21-22.

Changes followed rapidly, however. On the New Orleans route, sleeping car service was dropped for good on September 25, 1967. Daylight Trains 23-24 were discontinued on July 11,

Below: Mail and express cars stretch out of sight as *Southerner* No. 8 winds through a cut south of Marshall, Texas in August, 1966. Somewhere back in the consist are a coach or two; a grill coach will be added to the bare-bones operation at Little Rock. *J. Parker Lamb*

Opposite page top: Once known as the *Ozarkers*, Trains 3 and 4 were secondary trains over the route between St. Louis and points in Arkansas and Texas. At 1:00pm on June 5, 1968, a forlorn No. 3 trudges out of St. Louis Union Station toward Fort Worth, where it will not arrive until 6:59 the following morning. Trains 3-4 were dropped on November 11, 1968. *Larry Thomas*

Opposite page bottom: *Texas Eagle* No. 42 waits at Houston Union Station for its 3:40pm departure time. By the time of this June 21, 1968 photo, the consist of the *Eagle* was down to a coach, diner-coach and a 14-4 sleeper to St. Louis. *Joe McMillan*

Below: A contrast in styles is apparent in this July, 1968 photo at New Orleans. IC E8 4020 and E6 4001 shine in the sunshine next to a rather grubby T&P E7 (note the outline of the missing nose eagle). Despite No. 6's "end is near" appearance, MoPac passenger service into New Orleans still included two daily arrivals and departures. *Harold K. Vollrath collection*

1968. Trains 21-22, the overnight coach-only remnants of the *Louisiana Eagle* survived into 1969, making their final runs on December 17. Their demise spelled the end of all Missouri Pacific passenger service into New Orleans.

An even more drastic change took place on January 1, 1969. On that day, after 110 years of storied service, the Pullman Company relinquished the operation of all remaining sleeping cars on all US railroads to the contracting carriers. Some roads, including Union Pacific, Santa Fe, and Illinois Central simply staffed the former Pullman cars with railroad crews; others, including GM&O and Missouri Pacific, responded by eliminating sleeper service throughout their entire systems.

A far cry from the multiple sections of the 1950's, or the 22-car leviathan that operated into the mid-1960's, the sad little train departing St. Louis on New Year's Day, 1969 consisted of three mail storage cars (one each for San Antonio, Houston and Fort Worth), three coaches and a St. Louis-San Antonio diner-lounge.

Following the loss of sleeping car service, the *Aztec Eagle* died without fanfare on January 16. Trains 41-42, the Houston section, were discontinued on April 2.

Trains 21-22, the Dallas-Fort Worth section, actually got sleeping cars back for a short while after January 1. The reason was that the railroad was paying sleeping car porters any-

way, and so sleepers returned to the train for the convenience of MoPac officials traveling between St. Louis and Dallas-Fort Worth.

With or without sleepers, however, Trains 21-22 were discontinued for good on May 31, 1969. The last run was widely noted in the media and among the railfan community, as the *Texas Eagle* was the last passenger train on any railroad to serve either Dallas or Fort Worth. The end was clearly at hand.

Trains 1-2 continued to operate with coaches and a dining car between St. Louis and San Antonio until September, 1970. At that time, the service was cut back to Texarkana, and a grill coach was substituted for the full diner. The proud *Texas Eagle* that began as matched 14-car streamliner pairs ended its days as a nameless one- or two-car consist hauled by a single E-unit between St. Louis and the Texas-Arkansas border.

Sample consist of Train No. 21, the *Texas Eagle*, at Little Rock, Arkansas, Jan. 31, 1955: MP E7A 2005; T&P E7A 2013; MP mail-storage 701; T&P mail-storage 100; MP baggage-dormitory 804; MP coach 868; T&P deluxe coach 458; MP dome-coach 894; MP diner 840; 5 bedroom lounge *Eagle Cliff*; 14-1-2 Pullman *Eagle Circle*; 14-1-2 Pullman *Eagle Domain*; 14-4 Pullman *Eagle Trail*; MP divided coach 867; 14-4 Pullman *Eagle Rock*.

11 Diesel Passenger Power Roster

The following roster includes Missouri Pacific Lines diesel powered passenger locomotives, including models purchased for freight service but delivered with steam generators or that had steam generators added.

Also included are T&P F7A and F7B units 1500-1501, 1581-82 and 1531B-1534B. These units were not originally equipped with steam generators, but were regeared for passenger service during the 1950's. With the exception of F7A No. 1501, the modified T&P F-units were also repainted into the *Eagle* color scheme found on MoPac-T&P EMD E-units. C&EI passenger power is included following the MoPac section, though it should be noted that only E9A 1102:2 was still on C&EI's roster when that road was merged into the MoPac and the line sale to the Louisville & Nashville was completed.

Roster sources include *Extra 2200 South*, the Missouri Pacific Historical Society, Joe Collias, Ray Curl, Charlie Duckworth, John Eagan, Jerry Michels, and Bruce Murray. The roster was compiled and edited by Kevin EuDaly, originally for *Missouri Pacific Diesel Power*, also available from White River Productions.

Alco-GE FA-2   1,600 hp   13 units
Wheels = 40"   Fuel = 1,200
Engine: Alco 244-D V-type 12-cylinder 4-cycle Turbocharged
74:18 Gearing   65 mph Max
373A was equipped with a 244-G engine
Traded in to EMD on GP18's MP-400-499 and scrapped

1st No	2nd No	Built	Build #	Notes & Dispositions
MP-361:1		01/52	79463	Retired 1961
MP-362:1		01/52	79464	Retired 1961
MP-363:1		01/52	79465	Retired 1961
MP-364:1		01/52	79466	Retired 1961
MP-365:1		01/52	79467	Retired 1961
MP-366:1		01/52	79468	Retired 1961
MP-367:1		01/52	79469	Retired 1961
MP-368:1		01/52	79470	Retired 1961
MP-369:1		01/52	79471	Retired 1961
MP-370:1	MP-1370:1	01/52	79707	Retired 1961
MP-371:1		01/52	79708	Retired 1961
MP-372:1		01/52	79709	Retired 1961
MP-373:1		08/53	80008	Retired 1962

Alco-GE FA-2   1,600 hp   6 units
Wheels = 40"   Fuel = 1,200
Engine: Alco 244-G V-type 12-cylinder 4-cycle Turbocharged
Min Speed for TE = 9.0 mph
74:18 Gearing   65 mph Max
Retired 1962, Traded in to EMD on GP18's MP-400-499, scrapped

1st No	2nd No	Built	Build#
MP-387	MP-1387:1	03/54	80831
MP-388	MP-1388:1	03/54	80832
MP-389	MP-1389:1	04/54	80833
MP-390	MP-1390:1	04/54	80834
MP-391	MP-1391:1	04/54	80895
MP-392	MP-1392:1	04/54	80896

EMD F3 series   1,500 hp   12 units
Wheels = 40"   Fuel = 1,200
Engine: EMD 16-567B V-type 16-cylinder 2-cycle
62:15 Gearing   65 mph Max

1st No	2nd No	Built	Build #	Notes & Dispositions
MP-561:1	MP-765:1	08/48	5417	Retired 1968, scrapped
MP-561B	MP-801B	08/48	5429	Retired 1970-1971, T-I to EMD
MP-562:1	MP-766:1	08/48	5419	Retired 1968, scrapped
MP-562B	MP-802B	08/48	5430	Retired 1968-1970, T-I to EMD
MP-563:1	MP-767:1	08/48	5421	Retired 1968, T-I to GE
MP-563B	MP-803B	08/48	5431	Retired 1968-1970, T-I to EMD
MP-564:1	MP-768:1	08/48	5423	Retired 1968, T-I to GE
MP-564B	MP-804B	08/48	5432	Retired 1970-1971, T-I to EMD
MP-565	MP-769:1	08/48	5425	Retired 1966, T-I to EMD
MP-565B	MP-805B	08/48	5433	Retired 1970-1971, T-I to EMD
MP-566	MP-770:1	08/48	5427	Retired 1966, T-I to EMD
MP-566B	MP-806B	08/48	5434	Retired 1970-1971, T-I to EMD

EMD "F5"   1,500 hp   8 units
Wheels = 40"   Fuel = 1,200
Engine: EMD 16-567B V-type 16-cylinder 2-cycle
62:15 Gearing   65 mph Max

1st No	2nd No	Built	Build#	Notes & Dispositions
MP-567	MP-771:1	09/48	5435	Retired 1968, T-I to GE, scrapped

EMD "F5" (Continued)

MP-567B	MP-807B	09/48	5439	Retired 03/71, T-I to EMD on SD40's, scrapped
MP-568	MP-772:1	09/48	5436	Retired 1968, T-I to GE, scrapped
MP-568B	MP-808B	09/48	5440	Retired 04/71, scrapped
MP-569	MP-773:1	09/48	5437	Retired 1968, T-I to GE, scrapped
MP-569B	MP-809B	09/48	5441	Retired 1968-1970, T-I to GE, scrapped
MP-570	MP-774:1	09/48	5438	Retired 1966, T-I to EMD, scrapped
MP-570B	MP-810B	09/48	5442	Retired 1970-1971, T-I to EMD, scrapped

EMD F7A   1,500 hp   10 units
Wheels = 40"   Fuel = 1,200
Engine: EMD 16-567B V-type 16-cylinder 2-cycle
62:15 Gearing   65 mph Max   All scrapped

1st No	2nd No	3rd No	Built	Build#	Retired	Dispositions
IGN-603	MP-822	MP-1822:1	09/49	7968	03/73	T-I to EMD
IGN-604	MP-823		09/49	7969	1970-71	T-I to EMD
IGN-605	MP-824	MP-1824:1	09/49	7970	02/72	T-I to EMD
IGN-606	MP-825		09/49	7971	02/72	T-I to EMD
STLB&M-611	MP-830	MP-1830	10/49	8006	05/73	T-I to EMD
STLB&M-612	MP-831		10/49	8007	1970-71	T-I to EMD
STLB&M-613	MP-832		10/49	8008	1970-71	T-I to EMD
STLB&M-614	MP-833		10/49	8009	1971	T-I to GE
IGN-617	MP-785:1		04/50	8645	1970-71	T-I to EMD
IGN-618	MP-786:1		04/50	8646	02/71	T-I to EMD

EMD F7 series   1,500 hp   6 units
Wheels = 40"   Fuel = 1,200
Engine: EMD 16-567B V-type 16-cylinder 2-cycle
62:15 Gearing   65 mph Max   All T-I to EMD

1st No	2nd No	3rd No	Built	Build#	Notes & Dispositions
T&P-1500	T&P-850:1	T&P-1850	02/49	8428	Retired 3/73, scrapped
T&P-1501	T&P-851:1	T&P-1851	11/49	8429	Retired 1971
T&P-1531B	T&P-881B		01/52	15841	Retired 2/73
T&P-1532B	T&P-882B		01/52	15842	Retired 1972 scrapped
T&P-1533B	T&P-883B		01/52	15843	Retired 1967-73, scrapped
T&P-1534B	T&P-884B		01/52	15844	Retired 1/73

EMD E7A   2,000 hp   10 units
Wheels = 36"   Fuel = 1,200
Engine: Two EMD 12-567A V-type 12-cylinder 2-cycle
55:22 Gearing   98 mph Max
Later regeared to 57:20 85 mph Max

1st No	2nd No	Built	Build#	Notes & Dispositions
T&P-2000:1	T&P-1	03/47	3767	Scrapped, 03/67
T&P-2001:1	T&P-2	03/47	3768	Scrapped, 03/67
T&P-2002	T&P-3	03/47	3936	Scrapped, 01/68
T&P-2003	T&P-4	03/47	3937	Scrapped, 11/68
T&P-2004	T&P-5	03/47	3938	Scrapped, 08/68
T&P-2005	T&P-6	03/47	3939	Scrapped, 08/68
T&P-2006	T&P-7	03/47	3940	T-I to EMD 01/69
T&P-2007	T&P-8	03/47	3941	Scrapped, 08/69
T&P-2008	T&P-9	04/49	8464	Scrapped, 08/68
T&P-2009	T&P-10	04/49	8465	Scrapped, 08/67

EMD E8A   2,250 hp   9 units
Wheels = 36"   Fuel = 1,200
Engine: Two EMD 12-567B V-type 12-cylinder 2-cycle
57:20 Gearing   85 mph Max
"Straight" passenger style pilot

1st No	2nd No	Built	Build#	Notes
B&M-3821	MP-42	01/50	9088	Note 1
T&P-2010	T&P-30	08/51	14548	Note 2
T&P-2011	T&P-31	08/51	14549	Note 3
T&P-2012	T&P-32	08/51	14557	Note 3
T&P-2013	T&P-33	08/51	14558	Note 2
T&P-2014	T&P-34	08/51	11584	Note 3
T&P-2015	T&P-35	08/51	11585	Note 2
T&P-2016	T&P-36	08/51	11586	Note 4
T&P-2017	T&P-37	08/51	11587	Note 4

Note 1: Bought from Boston & Maine 06/62. Retired 1972, T-I to EMD on GP38-2's, scrapped
Note 2: Retired 3/70, T-I to EMD on SD40's, scrapped
Note 3: Retired 4/69, T-I to GE on U30C's, scrapped
Note 4: Retired 1/70, T-I to EMD on SD40's, scrapped

EMC NW4   900 hp   2 units
Wheels = 38"   Fuel = 600
Engine: Winton 12-201A V-type 12-cylinder 2-cycle
59:18 Gearing for 4102 77 mph Max
59:17 Gearing for 4103 77 mph Max

1st No	2nd No	Built	Build#	Notes & Dispositions
EMC-823	MP-4102	08/38	823	Retired 2/61, scrapped
EMC-824	MP-4103	08/38	824	Retired 3/61, scrapped

EMD GP7   1,500 hp   8 units
Wheels = 40"   Fuel = 800
Engine: EMD 16-567B V-type 16-cylinder 2-cycle
62:15 Gearing   65 mph Max
Upgraded to 1,600 hp   All T-I to EMD

1st No	2nd No	3rd No	4th No	Built	Build#	Retired	Notes
MP-4142	MP-295			07/50	8670	1979	Note 1
MP-4143	MP-296			07/50	8671	12/79	Note 2
MP-4144	MP-297			07/50	8672	9/79	Note 1
MP-4145	MP-298			07/50	8673	1975-79	Note 1
MP-4146	MP-299	MP-332:3	MP-1753	07/50	8674	8/81	Note 3
MP-4147	MP-300	MP-1750		07/50	8675	1980	Note 4
MP-4148	MP-301:2	MP-1751		07/50	8676	12/75	Note 4, 5
MP-4149	MP-302:2	MP-1752		07/50	8677	1979-81	Note 4

Note 1: T-I to EMD
Note 2: T-I to EMD on GP38-2's MP-2158-2197
Note 3: Rebuilt to "GP7u," chopnose by MoPac. T-I to EMD
Note 4: Rebuilt to "GP7u," 1,800 hp 567BC engine, snow plow front, chopnose by MoPac, 2,500 gallon fuel tank. T-I to EMD
Note 5: Wrecked at Vienna IL 6/12/75, T-I to EMD

EMD GP7   1,500 hp   16 units
Wheels = 40"   Fuel = 800
Engine: EMD 16-567B V-type 16-cylinder 2-cycle
62:15 Gearing   65 mph Max
Upgraded to 1,600 hp
Units rebuilt to "GP7u" had 1,800 hp EMD 16-567BC engine, snow plow front, chopnose by MoPac, and 2,500 gallon fuel tank.

1st No	2nd No	3rd No	4th No	Built	Build#	Notes
MP-4150	MP-303:2	MP-1754		05/51	14350	Note 1, 2
MP-4151	MP-304:2	MP-1755		05/51	14351	Note 1, 3
MP-4152	MP-305:2	MP-1756		05/51	14352	Note 1, 4
IGN-4153	MP-157:2	MP-257:2	MP-1725	03/51	14330	Note 5
IGN-4154	MP-158			03/51	14331	Note 6
IGN-4155	MP-159			03/51	14332	Note 7
IGN-4156	MP-160			03/51	14333	Note 6
IGN-4157	MP-161			03/51	14334	Note 6
IGN-4158	MP-162			03/51	14335	Note 8
STLB&M-4159	MP-163			04/51	14320	Note 9
STLB&M-4160	MP-164			04/51	14321	Note 6
STLB&M-4161	MP-306:2	MP-1757		04/51	14322	Note 1, 7
STLB&M-4162	MP-307:2	MP-1758		04/51	14323	Note 1, 5
STLB&M-4163	MP-308:2	MP-1759		04/51	14324	Note 1, 10
STLB&M-4164	MP-165			04/51	14318	Note 8
STLB&M-4165	MP-166			04/51	14319	Note 11

EMD GP7 (Continued)
Note 1: Rebuilt to "GP7u."
Note 2: Retired 8/81, T-I to EMD
Note 3: Wrecked 2/3/76 Ward AR, T-I to EMD
Note 4: Retired 11/81, T-I to EMD
Note 5: Retired 1979-1981, T-I to EMD
Note 6: Retired 1975-1979, T-I to EMD
Note 7: Retired 9/79, T-I to EMD
Note 8: Retired 12/79, T-I to EMD on GP38-2's MP-2158-2197
Note 9: Snow plow front. Chopnose by MoPac. Retired 1976, T-I to EMD
Note 10: Retired 1/76, T-I to EMD
Note 11: Retired 11/74, T-I to EMD

EMD GP7   1,500 hp   11 units
Wheels = 40"   Fuel = 800
Engine: EMD 16-567B V-type 16-cylinder 2-cycle
62:15 Gearing   65 mph Max
All but 4249 rebuilt to "GP7u" with Chopnose by MoPac snow plow front, 2,500 gallon fuel tank, and 1,800 hp.
Exceptions: 1764 had no snow plow
1766 not chopnose and no snow plow
1681 not chopnose, no snow plow, and 1,800 gallon fuel tank
All T-I to EMD

1st No	2nd No	3rd No	4th No	Built	Build#	Retired	Notes
MP-4241	MP-309:2	MP-1760		05/52	16165	79-81	
MP-4242	MP-310:2	MP-1761		05/52	16166	11/81	
MP-4243	MP-311:2	MP-1762		05/52	16167	08/81	
MP-4244	MP-312:2	MP-1763		05/52	16168	08/81	
MP-4245	MP-238	MP-1680:1	MP-1764	05/52	16169	79-81	
MP-4246	MP-313:2	MP-1765		05/52	16170	1980	Note 1
MP-4247	MP-314:2	MP-1766		05/52	16171	08/81	
MP-4248	MP-315:2			05/52	16172	08/81	
STLB&M-4249	MP-239	MP-1681:1		04/52	16123	79-81	
STLB&M-4250	MP-316:2	MP-1767		04/52	16124	1980	
STLB&M-4251	MP-317:2	MP-1768		04/52	16125	08/81	

Note 1: Wrecked 4/2/71 at Paola, rebuilt

EMD GP7   1,500 hp   4 units
Wheels = 40"   Fuel = 1,100
Engine: EMD 16-567B V-type 16-cylinder 2-cycle
62:15 Gearing   65 mph Max
Rebuilt to "GP7u," rerated to 1,800 hp, 2,500 gallon fuel tanks
All T-I to EMD

1st No	2nd No	3rd No	Built	Build#	Notes & Dispositions
STLB&M-4252	MP-318:2	MP-1769	03/53	18031	Note 1, retired 8/81
STLB&M-4253	MP-319:2	MP-1770	03/53	18032	Note 1, retired 1979-81
IGN-4254	MP-320:2	MP-1771	03/53	18026	Retired 1980
IGN-4255	MP-321:2	MP-1772	03/53	18027	Retired 1980

Note 1: Chopnose by MoPac, snow plow front.

EMD GP7   1,500 hp   5 units
Wheels = 40"   Fuel = 1,100
Engine: EMD 16-567B V-type 16-cylinder 2-cycle
62:15 Gearing   65 mph Max
Steam generators added
Rebuilt to "GP7u," rerated to 1,800 hp, 2,500 gallon fuel tanks

1st No	2nd No	3rd No	4th No	Built	Build#	Notes
MP-4256	MP-322:2	MP-1773		03/53	18021	Note 1
MP-4257	MP-323:2	MP-1774		03/53	18022	Note 1
MP-4258	MP-324:2	MP-1775		03/53	18023	Note 1
MP-4259	MP-325:2	MP-1776:1	MP-1639:1	03/53	18024	Note 2
MP-4260	MP-326:2	MP-1777		03/53	18025	Note 1, 3

Note 1: Retired 1979-1981, T-I to EMD
Note 2: Renumbered to make room for Bicentennial GP7 1776:2 (ex C&EI-84). Retired 11/75, T-I to EMD
Note 3: Chopnose by MoPac, snow plow front.

EMD GP7   1,500 hp   10 units
Wheels = 40"   Fuel = 1,100
Engine: EMD 16-567B V-type 16-cylinder 2-cycle
62:15 Gearing   65 mph Max
Rebuilt to "GP7u," rerated to 1,800 hp, 2,500 gallon fuel tanks. All T-I to EMD

1st No	2nd No	3rd No	Built	Build#	Retired	Notes
MP-4316	MP-327:2	MP-1778	03/54	19410	08/81	
MP-4317	MP-328:2	MP-1779	03/54	19411	1980	

EMD GP7 (Continued)

MP-4318	MP-329:2	MP-1780	03/54	19412	08/81	
MP-4319	MP-330:2	MP-1781	03/54	19413	08/81	
MP-4320	MP-331:2	MP-1782	03/54	19414	79-81	Note 1, 2
MP-4321	MP-332:2		04/54	19415	1974	Note 1, 2, 3
MP-4322	MP-333:2	MP-1783	04/54	19416	1980	
STLB&M-4323	MP-334:2	MP-1784	04/54	19426	79-81	Note 1, 2
STLB&M-4324	MP-335:2	MP-1785	04/54	19427	1980	Note 1, 2
IGN-4325	MP-336:2	MP-1786	05/54	19417	79-81	Note 1

Note 1: Chopnose by MoPac
Note 2: Snow plow front
Note 3: 567BC engine

EMC-GE E3A 2,000 hp 2 units
Wheels = 36" Fuel = 1,200
Engine: Two EMC 567 V-type 12-cylinder 2-cycle
55:22 Gearing 98 mph Max
Retired 5/62, scrapped

1st No	Built	Build#
MP-7000	10/39	936
MP-7001	10/39	937

EMD E6 series 2,000 hp 4 units
Wheels = 36" Fuel = 1,200
Engine: Two EMD 12-567 V-type 12-cylinder 2-cycle
55:22 Gearing 98 mph Max

1st No	2nd No	Built	Build#	Dispositions
MP-7002	MP-11	10/41	1389	Scrapped
MP-7002B	MP-11B	10/41	1391	Scrapped
MP-7003	MP-12	10/41	1390	Scrapped
MP-7003B	MP-12B	10/41	1392	Scrapped

EMD E7 2,000 hp 22 units
Wheels = 36" Fuel = 1,200
Engine: Two EMD 12-567A V-type 12-cylinder 2-cycle
55:22 Gearing 98 mph Max
MP-7004 A & B geared 52:25 with 117 mph max, regeared 55:22, 98 mph Max

1st No	2nd No	Built	Build#	Notes & Dispositions
MP-7004	MP-13	09/45	2895	Scrapped
MP-7004B	MP-13B	09/45	2896	Scrapped
MP-7005	MP-14	02/47	3762	Scrapped
MP-7006	MP-15:1	03/47	3763	Scrapped
IGN-7007	MP-16:1	03/47	3766	Scrapped
STLB&M-7008	MP-17:1	03/47	3887	Scrapped
STLB&M-7009	MP-18:1	03/47	3888	Scrapped
MP-7010	MP-19:1	02/47	3758	Scrapped
MP-7010B	MP-14B	02/47	3760	Scrapped
MP-7011	MP-20:1	02/47	3759	Retired 8/67, to PNC, to L&N-754
MP-7011B	MP-15B	02/47	3761	Scrapped
IGN-7012	MP-21:1	03/47	3764	Retired 8/67, to PNC, to L&N (parts)
IGN-7012B	MP-16B	03/47	3765	Scrapped
IGN-7013	MP-22:1	09/47	4795	T-I to EMD
MP-7014	MP-23:1	06/48	5443	Retired 5/70, T-I to EMD
MP-7014B	MP-17B	06/48	5447	Scrapped
MP-7015	MP-24:1	06/48	5444	Retired 1968-1970, T-I to EMD
MP-7015B	MP-18B	06/48	5448	Scrapped
MP-7016	MP-25:1	06/48	5445	Scrapped
MP-7016B	MP-19B	06/48	5449	Scrapped
MP-7017	MP-26:1	06/48	5446	Retired 1968-1970, T-I to EMD
MP-7017B	MP-20B	06/48	5450	Scrapped

EMD E8A 2,250 hp 4 units
Wheels = 36" Fuel = 1,200
Engine: Two EMD 12-567B V-type 12-cylinder 2-cycle
55:22 Gearing 98 mph Max
T-I to EMD on GP38-2's

1st No	2nd No	Built	Build#	Notes & Dispositions
MP-7018	MP-38	06/50	8635	Retired 1/72, scrapped
MP-7019	MP-39	06/50	8636	Retired 5/72, scrapped
MP-7020	MP-40	06/50	8637	Retired 5/72, to Pielet, scrapped
MP-7021	MP-41	06/50	8638	Retired 5/72, scrapped

EMC AA6 (1/2 of an E6) 1,000 hp 1 unit
Wheels = 36" Fuel = 1,200
Engine: EMC 567 V-type 12-cylinder 2-cycle
55:22 Gearing 98 mph Max
Last Motorcar built by EMC

1st No	Built	Build#	Notes & Disposition
MP-7100	08/40	1082	Retired 2/62, scrapped

Alco-GE PA-1 2,000 hp 8 units
TE = 52,620 WT = 315,730 (210,490 on powered wheels)
Wheels = 40" Fuel = 1,200
Engine: Alco 244-C V-type 16-cylinder 4-cycle Turbocharged
Min Speed for TE = 23.0 mph
60:23 Gearing 100 mph Max

1st No	2nd No	Built	Build#	Notes & Dispositions
MP-8001:1	MP-44	10/49	77503	Retired 1966, T-I to EMD
MP-8002:1	MP-45	10/49	77504	Retired 1966, T-I to EMD
MP-8003:1	MP-46	10/49	77505	Retired 1966, T-I to EMD
MP-8004:1	MP-47	10/49	77506	Retired 1966, T-I to EMD
MP-8005:1	MP-48	11/49	77507	Retired 1966, T-I to EMD
MP-8006:1	MP-49	11/49	77508	Retired 1964-1965, to PNC
MP-8007:1	MP-50	11/49	77509	Retired 1964-1965, to PNC
MP-8008	MP-51	11/49	77510	Retired 1964-1965, to PNC

Alco-GE PA-2 2,250 hp 4 units
TE = 52,600 WT = 315,570 (210,380 on powered wheels)
Wheels = 40" Fuel = 1,200
Engine: Alco 244-C V-type 16-cylinder 4-cycle Turbocharged
Min Speed for TE = 21.0 mph
60:23 Gearing 100 mph Max

1st No	2nd No	Built	Build#	Notes & Dispositions
MP-8009	MP-52	05/50	78135	Retired 1964-1965, to Chandeysson Electric
MP-8010	MP-53	05/50	78136	Retired 4/65, to PNC
IGN-8011	MP-54	06/50	78137	Retired 1966, T-I to EMD
IGN-8012	MP-55	06/50	78138	Retired 4/65, to Chandeysson Electric

Alco-GE PA-2 2,250 hp 6 units
TE = 52,800 WT = 316,800 (211,200 on powered wheels)
Wheels = 40" Fuel = 1,200
Engine: Alco 244-C V-type 16-cylinder 4-cycle Turbocharged
Min Speed for TE = 21.0 mph
60:23 Gearing 100 mph Max

1st No	2nd No	Built	Build#	Notes & Dispositions
MP-8013	MP-56	05/51	78734	Retired 1966, T-I to EMD
MP-8014	MP-57	05/51	78735	Retired 5/64, to Chandeysson Electric
MP-8015	MP-58	06/51	78736	Retired 1966, T-I to EMD
MP-8016	MP-59	06/51	78737	Retired 4/65, to PNC
MP-8017	MP-60	06/51	78738	Retired 5/64, to Chandeysson Electric
MP-8018	MP-61	06/51	78739	Retired 1966, to EMD

Alco-GE PA-3 2,250 hp 18 units
TE = 53,180 WT = 319,050 (212,700 on powered wheels)
Wheels = 40" Fuel = 1,200
Engine: Alco 244-D V-type 16-cylinder 4-cycle Turbocharged
Min Speed for TE = 21.0 mph
60:23 Gearing 100 mph Max

1st No	2nd No	Built	Build#	Notes & Dispositions
MP-8019	MP-62	05/52	79042	Retired 5/64, to Chandeysson Electric
MP-8020	MP-63	05/52	79043	Retired 5/64, to Chandeysson Electric
MP-8021	MP-64	06/52	79044	Retired 4/65, to PNC
MP-8022	MP-65	06/52	79045	Retired 5/64, to Chandeysson Electric
MP-8023	MP-66	06/52	78208	Retired 5/64, to Chandeysson Electric
MP-8024	MP-67	06/52	78209	Retired 5/64, to Chandeysson Electric
MP-8025	MP-68:1	06/52	78210	Retired 5/64, to Chandeysson Electric
MP-8026	MP-69:1	06/52	78211	Wore Jenks blue as MP-8026. Retired 5/64, to Chandeysson Electric
MP-8027	MP-70:1	07/52	78957	Retired 5/64, to Chandeysson Electric
MP-8028	MP-71:1	07/52	78958	Retired 4/65, to PNC
MP-8029	MP-72:1	07/52	78959	Retired 5/64, to Chandeysson Electric
MP-8030	MP-73:1	08/52	78960	Retired 4/65, to PNC
MP-8031	MP-74:1	08/52	80045	Retired 5/64, to Chandeysson Electric
MP-8032	MP-75:1	08/52	80046	Wore Jenks blue as MP-8032. Retired 4/65, to PNC
MP-8033	MP-76:1	08/52	80047	Retired 5/64, to Chandeysson Electric

MP-8034 MP-77:1 08/52   80048   Retired 5/64, to Chandeysson Electric
MP-8035 MP-78:1 08/52   80049   Retired 1966, T-I to EMD
MP-8036 MP-79:1 09/52   80050   Retired 1966, T-I to EMD

Chicago & Eastern Illinois Passenger Power

EMD E7A   2,000 hp   3 units
Wheels = 36"   Fuel = 1,200
Engine: Two EMD 12-567A V-type 12-cylinder 2-cycle
55:22 Gearing   98 mph Max

1st No	2nd No	3rd No	Built	Build#	Notes
C&EI-1100	C&EI-27	L&N-798	05/46	3374	Note 1
C&EI-1101	C&EI-28	L&N-799	05/46	3375	Note 1
C&EI-1102:1			09/46	3585	Note 2

Note 1: Transferred to L&N 2/7/68. Retired by L&N 1971
Note 2: Wrecked in 1958, T-I on "E9Am" C&EI-1102:2

EMD "E9Am"   2,400 hp   1 unit
Wheels = 36"   Fuel = 1,200
Engine: Two EMD 12-567B V-type 12-cylinder 2-cycle
57:20 Gearing   85 mph Max

1st No	2nd No	Built	Build#	Notes & Disposition
C&EI-1102:2	C&EI-43	08/58	24733	Note 1

Note 1: Rebuilt from wrecked E7A C&EI-1102:1. Retired 4/72, T-I to EMD on GP38-2's, to Pielet, scrapped

EMD F3A   1,500 hp   4 units
Wheels = 40"   Fuel = 1,200
Engine: EMD 16-567B 16-cylinder 2-cycle
59:18 Gearing   83 mph Max
T-I to EMD on GP35's, scrapped

1st No	Built	Build#	Notes
C&EI-1200	02/48	6018	Retired 8/64
C&EI-1201	02/48	6019	Retired 7/64
C&EI-1202:1	02/48	6020	Retired 7/64
C&EI-1203:1	02/48	6021	Retired 9/64

EMD F3A   1,500 hp   2 units
Wheels = 40"   Fuel = 1,200
Engine: EMD 16-567B 16-cylinder 2-cycle
59:18 Gearing   83 mph Max
T-I to EMD on GP35's, scrapped

1st No	Built	Build#	Notes
C&EI-1204:1	02/49	6004	Retired 8/64
C&EI-1205:1	02/49	6005	Retired 8/64

EMD F3B   1,500 hp   2 units
Wheels = 40"   Fuel = 1,200
Engine: EMD 16-567B 16-cylinder 2-cycle
59:18 Gearing   83 mph Max
Steam generator added 1949
Retired 11/64, T-I to EMD on GP35's, scrapped

1st No	Built	Build#
C&EI-1300	02/48	6022
C&EI-1301	02/48	6023

EMD F3A   1,500 hp   4 units
Wheels = 40"   Fuel = 1,200
Engine: EMD 16-567B 16-cylinder 2-cycle
62:15 Gearing   65 mph Max
Steam generator added 1949
Rerated to 1,600 hp
T-I to EMD on GP35's, scrapped

1st No	Built	Build#	Notes & Dispositions
C&EI-1400	07/48	6006	Retired 11/63
C&EI-1401	07/48	6007	Retired 12/63
C&EI-1402	07/48	6008	Retired 11/63
C&EI-1403	07/48	6009	Retired 6/64

EMD F3B   1,500 hp   2 units
Wheels = 40"   Fuel = 1,200
Engine: EMD 16-567B 16-cylinder 2-cycle
62:15 Gearing   65 mph Max
Steam generator added 1949

1st No	2nd No	3rd No	Built	Build#	Notes & Dispositions
C&EI-1500			07/48	6010	Retired 9/64, T-I to EMD on GP35's, scrapped
C&EI-1501	C&EI-750B	C&EI-933B	07/48	6011	Retired 3/73, scrapped

EMD F3A ("F5A")   1,500 hp   6 units
Wheels = 40"   Fuel = 1,200
Engine: EMD 16-567B 16-cylinder 2-cycle
59:18 Gearing   83 mph Max
Steam generator added 1949
Rerated to 1,600 hp

1st No	2nd No	3rd No	Built	Build#	Retired	Notes
C&EI-1404			11/48	7850	09/64	Note 1
C&EI-1405	C&EI-750	C&EI-824	11/48	7851	04/72	Scrapped
C&EI-1406			12/48	5998	12/64	Note 1
C&EI-1407	C&EI-751	C&EI-827	12/48	5999	07/71	Note 2
C&EI-1408			12/48	6000	08/64	Note 1
C&EI-1409			12/48	6001	11/64	Note 1

Note 1: T-I to EMD on GP35's, scrapped
Note 2: To GE 07/71, scrapped

EMD F3B ("F5B")   1,500 hp   3 units
Wheels = 40"   Fuel = 1,200
Engine: EMD 16-567B 16-cylinder 2-cycle
59:18 Gearing   83 mph Max
Steam generators added 1949

1st No	2nd No	3rd No	Built	Build#	Notes & Dispositions
C&EI-1502	C&EI-751B	C&EI-934B	11/48	7852	Retired 1/72, scrapped
C&EI-1503	C&EI-752B	C&EI-935B	12/48	6002	Retired 8/72, scrapped
C&EI-1504	C&EI-753B	C&EI-936B	12/48	6003	Retired 1/72, scrapped

EMD BL2   1,500 hp   2 units
Wheels = 40"   Fuel = 500
Engine: EMD 16-567 16-cylinder 2-cycle
62:15 Gearing   65 mph Max
T-I 04/63 to EMD on GP30's C&EI-239-241

1st No	2nd No	Built	Build#
C&EI-1600:1	C&EI-200	12/48	6012
C&EI-1601:1	C&EI-201	12/48	6013

EMD BL1   1,500 hp   1 unit
Wheels = 40"   Fuel = 500
Engine: EMD 16-567 16-cylinder 2-cycle
62:15 Gearing   65 mph Max

1st No	2nd No	3rd No	Built	Build#	Notes
GM/EMD 499	C&EI-1602:1	C&EI-202	09/47	7428	Note 1

Note 1: T-I 02/63 to EMD on GP30's C&EI-239-241, scrapped

EMD FP7A   1,500 hp   10 units
Wheels = 40"   Fuel = 1,200
Engine: EMD 16-567B 16-cylinder 2-cycle
59:18 Gearing   83 mph Max
Steam generators added 1949

1st No	2nd No	3rd No	Built	Build#	Notes & Dispositions
C&EI-1600:2	C&EI-933	L&N-670	08/48	7535	Note 1, 3
C&EI-1601:2	C&EI-934	L&N-671	08/48	7536	Note 1
C&EI-1602:2	C&EI-935	L&N-672	08/48	7537	Note 1
C&EI-1603	C&EI-936	L&N-673	08/48	7538	Note 1
C&EI-1604	C&EI-937	L&N-674	08/48	7539	Note 1, 3
C&EI-1605	C&EI-938	L&N-675	09/48	7540	Note 1, 2
C&EI-1606	C&EI-939	L&N-676	09/48	7541	Note 1
C&EI-1607	C&EI-940	L&N-677	09/48	7542	Note 1, 3
C&EI-1608	C&EI-941	C&EI-1941	09/48	7543	Retired 3/74, T-I to EMD
C&EI-1609	C&EI-942		09/48	7544	Retired 11/71, T-I to EMD

Note 1: Transferred to L&N 2/7/68
Note 2: Retired by L&N 1970
Note 3: Retired by L&N 1971

Listed below are all known streamlined passenger-carrying equipment owned by the Missouri Pacific, Texas & Pacific, and Gulf Coast Lines, as well as cars transferred to Missouri Pacific ownership following the acquisition of the Chicago & Eastern Illinois. Also included are mail, baggage and express cars built or rebuilt for passenger service. (e.g., express-box, etc.).

Equipment listings are arranged according to the following sequence:

1. Car builder, in alphabetical order;
2. Car type-generally from the front to the rear of the train, e.g., head-end cars, coaches, food service cars, first-class cars;
3. First Missouri Pacific Lines road number assigned, regardless of original car ownership;
4. Sleeping cars not numbered at the time of purchase are listed in order of first numbering after 1962;

5. Cars may be combined with other sequentially numbered cars if all relevant data are identical. Cars within a given grouping having dissimilar characteristics, e.g., different retirement dates, are identified separately.

"Car type" indicates car configuration at the time of retirement, sale or scrappage. Information regarding rebuilding or reconfiguration is shown in footnotes within each section. No equipment appears in more than one listing.

Equipment Built by American Car and Foundry (ACF)

Self Propelled Motor Trains

Owner	Original Number	Car Type	Date Built	Date Retired	Final Number
MP	670	MotoRailer	1942	1961	670

Head-End Cars

Owner	Original Number	Car Type	Date Built	Date Retired	Final Number
T&P	100-103	Mail-Baggage	1948	1968	382-385
T&P	104	Mail-Baggage	1948	1969	386
D&H	420	Baggage	1957	1969	310(1)
D&H	419	Baggage	1957	1970	311(1)
D&H	404	Baggage	1957	1969	312(1)
D&H	402	Baggage	1957	1969	313(1)
D&H	414	Baggage	1957	1969	314(1)
D&H	410	Baggage	1957	1969	315(1)
D&H	403	Baggage	1957	1968	316(1)
D&H	418	Baggage	1957	1969	317(1)
D&H	406	Baggage	1957	1969	318(1)
D&H	409	Baggage	1957	1969	319(1)
T&P	300-301	Bagg.-Dorm	1948	1970	360-361
T&P	302	Bagg.-Dorm	1948	1962	362
T&P	303-304	Bagg.-Dorm	1948	1968	363-364
MP	700	Baggage	1940	1967	350
MP	701	Baggage	1940	1969	351
MP	710-711	Mail-Baggage	1940	1968	370-371
MP	804	Bagg.-Dorm	1948	1968	365
MP	810-812	Mail-Baggage	1948	1968	374-376
IGN	813	Mail-Baggage	1948	1962	377
IGN	814-815	Mail-Baggage	1948	1968	378-379
SLBM	816-817	Mail-Baggage	1948	1968	380-381
MP	2400-2401	Mail-Storage	1960	1969	300-301
MP	2402	Mail-Storage	1960	1962	302
MP	2403-2404	Mail-Storage	1960	1969	303-304
MP	2405	Mail-Storage	1960	1971	305
MP	2406-2409	Mail-Storage	1960	1969	306-309

(1) Baggage cars 310-319 acquired from Delaware & Hudson, 1962. Originally renumbered 250-259.

Coaches

Owner	Original Number	Car Type	Date Built	Date Retired	Final Number
T&P	400-401	Dlx. Divided	1948	1969	475-476
T&P	450	Dlx. Coach	1948	1969	450
T&P	451	Dlx. Coach	1948	1970	451
T&P	452	Dlx. Coach	1948	1962	452
T&P	453-460	Dlx. Coach	1948	1969	453-460
MP	720-721	Coach	1940	1966	400-401
MP	730	Dlx. Coach	1940	1966	477
MP	731	Dlx. Coach	1940	1968	478
MP	820	Coach Dorm.	1948	1969	420
MP	821	Coach Dorm.	1948	1968	521

Coaches (Continued)

Owner	Original Number	Car Type	Date Built	Date Retired	Final Number
IGN	822-823	Coach Dorm.	1948	1967	522-523
MP	830	Dlx. Coach	1948	1969	489
SLBM	850-853	Dlx. Stateroom	1948	1969	494-497
SLBM	854	Dlx. Stateroom	1948	1968	498
SLBM	855	Dlx. Stateroom	1948	1969	499
MP	863	Dlx. Divided	1948	1971	468
MP	864-867	Dlx. Divided	1948	1969	469-472
IGN	868	Dlx. Divided	1948	1969	473
IGN	869	Dlx. Divided	1948	1971	474

Food Service Cars

Owner	Original Number	Car Type	Date Built	Date Retired	Final Number
T&P	480-481	Grill Coach	1948	1973	569-570
T&P	500	Diner	1948	1967	30
T&P	525-526	Diner-Lounge	1948	1969	42-43
T&P	527	Diner-Lounge	1948	1966	44
MP	740-741	Diner-Lounge	1940	1965	34-35
SLBM	824	Grill Coach	1948	1967	571
SLBM	825	Grill Coach	1948	1970	572
MP	840	Diner	1948	1967	31
MP	841-842	Diner Coach	1948	1974	580-581(1)
MP	843	Diner-Lounge	1948	1965	38
IGN	844	Diner-Lounge	1948	1965	39
IGN	845	Diner-Lounge	1948	1969	40
MP	870-873	Grill Coach	1948	1968	564-567
IGN	874	Grill Coach	1948	1968	568

(1) Purchased as diner-lounge cars. Converted to coach-diner cars after 1961.

Parlor Cars

Owner	Original Number/Name	Car Type	Date Built	Date Retired	Final Number
MP	750	Parlor-Obs.	1940	1962	750
MP	751	Parlor-Obs.	1940	1962	751

Equipment Built by the Budd Company

Self Propelled Motor Trains

Owner	Original Number/Name	Car Type	Date Built	Date Retired	Final Number
T&P	100	Mtr. Mail Bag.	1933	1934	100
T&P	150	Trlr. Coach	1933	1934	150

Head-End Cars

Owner	Original Number/Name	Car Type	Date Built	Date Retired	Final Number
MP	702-704	Baggage	1942	1968	350-352
MP	712-713	Mail-Baggage	1942	1968	372-373

Coaches

Owner	Original Number/Name	Car Type	Date Built	Date Retired	Final Number
T&P	461	Dlx. Coach	1949	1969	461

Equipment Built by the Budd Company (Continued)

Coaches (Continued)

Owner	Original Number/Name	Car Type	Date Built	Date Retired	Final Number
C&EI	475-478	Coach	1953	1969	440-443
C&EI	479-480	Coach	1953	1970	444-445
C&EI	481-482	Coach	1953	1969	446-447
C&EI	483	Coach	1953	1970	448
C&EI	484	Coach	1953	1969	449
MP	722	Coach Dorm.	1942	1969	524
MP	723	Coach Dorm.	1942	1968	525
MP	733-734	Dlx. Coach	1942	1968	479-480
IGN	831-832	Dlx. Coach	1949	1970	462-463
IGN	833	Dlx. Coach	1949	1968	464
MP	860	Dlx. Divided	1948		465(1)
MP	861-862	Dlx. Divided	1948	1971	466-467
MP	890-892	Dome Coach	1948	1967	590-592

(1) Coach 465 converted to air brake instruction car 20, 1971

Food Service Cars

Owner	Original Number/Name	Car Type	Date Built	Date Retired	Final Number
MP	742 *Cheyenne Mountain*	Diner-Lounge	1942	1969	36
MP	743 *San Isabel*	Diner-Lounge	1942	1969	37
IGN	846	Diner-Lounge	1949	1969	41
MP	847	Diner Coach	1949	1974	582(1)
C&O	1702 *Harvest Inn*	Tavern	1948	1969	34(2)

(1) Purchased as diner-lounge car.
(2) Acquired from C&O by C&EI in 1951. Originally renumbered C&EI 475 after purchase from C&O. Later renumbered C&EI 703, then C&EI 34.

Sleeping Cars

Owner	Original Name	Car Type	Date Built	Date Retired	Final Number
MP	*Canyon River*	10-6	1949	1969	610
MP	*Crystal River*	10-6	1949		611(1)
MP	*Elk River*	10-6	1949	1983	612
MP	*Roaring River*	10-6	1949	1969	613
MP	*Eagle Butte*	10-6	1949	1969	614
MP	*Eagle Chasm*	10-6	1949	1983	615
MP	*Eagle Haven*	10-6	1956	1969	616(2)
MP	*Eagle Hollow*	10-6	1956	1969	617(2)
MP	*Eagle Lodge*	10-6	1956	1969	618(2)
MP	*Eagle Meadow*	10-6	1956	1969	619(2)
MP	*Eagle Rapids*	10-6	1956	1969	620(2)
MP	*Eagle View*	10-6	1956	1983	621(2)
MP	*Southland*	24 single/8 double room	1959	1964	699

(1) Converted to Business Car 11, 1971.
(2) Cars 616-621 delivered with 6 wheel trucks.

Equipment Built by Missouri Pacific DeSoto Shops

Owner	Original Number	Car Type	Date Built	Date Retired	Final Number
MP	135	Box-Express	1962	1968	135
MP	136-145	Box-Express	1962	1969	136-145
MP	146	Box-Express	1962	1968	146
MP	147-184	Box-Express	1962	1969	147-184

Equipment Built by Pullman-Standard

Head-End Cars

Owner	Original Number/Name	Car Type	Date Built	Date Retired	Final Number
T&P	1700-1724	Box-Express	1937	1965	100-124
T&P	642 *Eagle Ridge*	RPO	1948	1971	387(1)

(1) Purchased as 5 Bedroom-Lounge-Soda Fountain sleeper in 1948. Rebuilt as RPO/mail storage car, 1966.

Equipment Built by Pullman-Standard (Continued)

Coaches

Owner	Original Number/Name	Car Type	Date Built	Date Retired	Final Number
T&P	200	Dome Coach	1952	1967	597
MEC	240	Dlx. Coach	1947	1969	481(1)
MEC	242-244	Dlx. Coach	1947	1969	482-484(1)
MEC	245	Dlx. Coach	1947	1968	485(1)
MEC	246	Dlx. Coach	1947	1970	486(1)
MEC	241	Dlx. Coach	1947	1970	487(1)
MEC	247	Dlx. Coach	1947	1969	488(1)
MP	593-596	Dome Coach	1952	1967	593-596
C&O	1800	Dlx. Coach	1950	1969	490(2)
C&O	1801	Coach	1950	1969	491(2)
C&O	1802-1803	Coach	1950	1969	492-493(3)
MP	630 *Eagle Bridge*	Coach	1948	1971	402(4)
MP	634 *Eagle Village*	Coach	1948	1971	403(4)
MP	631 *Eagle Circle*	Coach	1948	1971	404(5)
T&P	635 *Eagle Flight*	Coach	1948	1971	405(4)
MP	632 *Eagle Country*	Coach	1948	1971	406(5)
T&P	682 *Eagle Watch*	Coach	1948	1971	407(6)
MP	633 *Eagle Glide*	Coach	1948	1971	408(5)
T&P	681 *Eagle Trail*	Coach	1948	1971	409(7)
MP	651 *Eagle Creek*	Coach	1948	1971	410(7)
MP	664 *Eagle Rock*	Coach	1948	1971	411(8)

(1) Acquired from Maine Central, 1960.
(2) Acquired from C&O, 1959.
(3) Acquired from C&O, 1959. Originally operated as parlor cars 87-88. Rebuilt as coaches 492-493, 1964.
(4) Purchased as 14-1-2 sleeper. Rebuilt as coach, 1964.
(5) Purchased as 14-1-2 sleeper. Rebuilt as coach, 1965.
(6) Purchased as 14-4 sleeper. Rebuilt as coach, 1965.
(7) Purchased as 14-4 sleeper. Rebuilt as coach, 1966.
(8) Purchased as 14-4 sleeper. Rebuilt as coach, 1967.

Food Service Cars

Owner	Original Number	Car Type	Date Built	Date Retired	Final Number
MEC	540	Grill Coach	1947	1974	562(1)
MEC	541	Grill Coach	1947	1969	563(1)

(1) Originally built as baggage-coaches. Converted to grill coaches and renumbered MP 761-762 at Sedalia Shops in 1960.

Sleeping Cars

Owner	Original Number/Name	Car Type	Date Built	Date Retired	Final Number
MP	*Arkansas River*	6-6-4	1941	1967	606
MP	*Colorado River*	6-6-4	1941	1967	607
MP	*Eagle River*	6-6-4	1941	1967	608
MP	*Gunnison River*	6-6-4	1941	1967	609
T&P	*Eagle Brook*	10-6	1948	1969	622(1)
T&P	*Eagle Country*	10-6	1948	1969	623(1)
T&P	*Eagle Domain*	10-6	1948	1969	624(1)
T&P	*Eagle Path*	10-6	1948	1969	625(1)
MP	*Eagle Cliff*	5 BR/Fntn.	1948	1967	640
MP	*Eagle Canyon*	5 BR/Fntn.	1948	1966	641
MP	*Eagle Chain*	14-4	1948	1969	650
MP	*Eagle Crest*	14-4	1948	1969	652
MP	*Eagle Dam*	14-4	1948	1969	653
MP	*Eagle Divide*	14-4	1948	1969	654
MP	*Eagle Forest*	14-4	1948	1969	655
IGN	*Eagle Height*	14-4	1948	1969	656
MP	*Eagle Hill*	14-4	1948	1969	657
MP	*Eagle Knob*	14-4	1948	1969	658
MP	*Eagle Lake*	14-4	1948	1969	659
MP	*Eagle Marsh*	14-4	1948	1961	(2)
MP	*Eagle Mountain*	14-4	1948	1969	660
MP	*Eagle Point*	14-4	1948	1969	661
IGN	*Eagle Preserve*	14-4	1948	1969	662
IGN	*Eagle Refuge*	14-4	1948	1969	663
MP	*Eagle Stream*	14-4	1948	1969	665
MP	*Eagle Summit*	14-4	1948	1969	666
IGN	*Eagle Tree*	14-4	1948	1969	667
MP	*Eagle Turn*	14-4	1948	1969	668

123

Equipment Built by Pullman-Standard (Continued)

Sleeping Cars (Continued)

Owner	Original Number/Name	Car Type	Date Built	Date Retired	Final Number
MP	*Eagle Valley*	14-4	1948	1969	669
MP	*Eagle Woods*	14-4	1948	1969	670
T&P	*Eagle Bay*	14-4	1948	1969	671
T&P	*Eagle Beach*	14-4	1948	1969	672
T&P	*Eagle Call*	14-4	1948	1969	673
T&P	*Eagle City*	14-4	1948	1969	674
T&P	*Eagle Island*	14-4	1948	1969	675
T&P	*Eagle Land*	14-4	1948	1969	676
T&P	*Eagle Light*	14-4	1948	1969	677
T&P	*Eagle Rest*	14-4	1948	1969	678
T&P	*Eagle Road*	14-4	1948	1969	679
T&P	*Eagle Spirit*	14-4	1948	1969	680
C&EI	902 *Loblolly Pine*	6-6-4	1967	1969	(3)

(1) T&P Cars *Eagle Brook*, *Eagle Country*, *Eagle Domain*, and *Eagle Path* originally built as 14-4 cars; converted to 10-6 cars by Pullman-Standard
(2) Car wrecked at Pine Bluff, Arkansas, prior to renumbering, 1961.
(3) Acquired with C&EI merger, 1967. Sold to L&N, 1969. Reacquired 1976 as Business Car No. 2.

Equipment Built by St. Louis Car Company

Head-End Cars

Owner	Original Name	Car Type	Date Built	Date Retired	Final Number
MP	200-249	Mail Storage	1964	1969	200-249
MP	250-276	Msngr. Bagg.	1965	1969	250-276
MP	277-279	Msngr. Bagg.	1965	1971	277-279
MP	280-299	Msngr. Bagg.	1965	1970	280-299

Equipment Built by St. Louis Car Company (Continued)

Food Service Cars

Owner	Original Number/Name	Car Type	Date Built	Date Retired	Final Number
MP	732	Grill Coach	1941	1965	560(1)
MP	760	Grill Coach	1941	1974	561

(1) Originally built as combination mail-coach. Converted to grill coach at Sedalia Shops in 1960.

Equipment Built by Texas & Pacific Marshall Shops

Owner	Original Number	Car Type	Date Built	Date Retired	Final Number
T&P	1725-1734	Box-Express	1954	1965	125-134

Abbreviations:

Bagg.	Baggage
C&EI	Chicago and Eastern Illinois
C&O	Chesapeake and Ohio
D&H	Delaware and Hudson
Dlx.	Deluxe
Dorm.	Dormitory
IGN	International-Great Northern
MEC	Maine Central
MP	Missouri Pacific
Msngr.	Messenger
Mtr.	Motor
Obs.	Observation
SLBM	St. Louis, Brownsville and Mexico
Trlr.	Trailer
T&P	Texas and Pacific

Pullman Car Types:

5 Br/Fntn	5 Double Bedroom Lounge-Soda Fountain
6-6-4	6 Section, 6 Roomette, 4 Double Bedroom
10-6	10 Roomette, 6 Double Bedroom
14-1-2	14 Roomette, 1 Drawing Room, 2 Double Bedroom
14-4	14 Roomette, 4 Double Bedroom

Bibliography

Adams, W. M., "High Bridges and Hard Rock Tunnels," *The Eagle*, Missouri Pacific Historical Society, (MPHS) October, 1974, p. 4.

Adams, W. M., "Some Consists of Missouri Pacific Passenger Trains on January 31, 1955, Little Rock Subdivision," MPHS collection.

Bennett, Jim, "Delta Eagle Commemoration," *The Eagle*, MPHS, Winter, 1991.

Boucher, Joel S., "Lightweight Passenger Car Fleet of the Missouri Pacific," *The Eagle*, MPHS, Spring, 1983.

Bryan, Frank W., "Milepost 150,000," Part IV, *The Eagle*, MPHS, June, 1974.

Chappuis, Camille F., "MoPac's C&EI Diesel Fleet," *The Eagle*, MPHS, Fall, 1984, p. 16.

Chicago and Eastern Illinois Railroad public timetables, 1946- 1968 (various).

Collias, Joe G., *The Missouri Pacific Lines in Color*, MM Books, Crestwood, MO, 1993.

Collias, Joe G., *The Texas & Pacific Railway--Super Power to Streamliners*, MM Books, Crestwood, MO, 1989.

Dolzall, Gary W., "The Case for the C&EI," *Trains Magazine*, Kalmbach Publishing Co., Milwaukee, WI, January, 1990, pp. 36-43.

Dubin, Arthur D., *More Classic Trains*, Kalmbach Publishing Co., Milwaukee, WI, 1974, p. 278.

Duckworth, Charles A, "The Eagle: Missouri Pacific's First Streamlined Train," *The Eagle*, MPHS, Spring, 1984.

Edmonson, Harold A., *Journey to Amtrak: The Year History Rode the Passenger Train*, Kalmbach Publishing Co., Milwaukee, WI, 1972, pp. 102-104.

EuDaly, Kevin N., *Missouri Pacific Diesel Power*, White River Productions, Kansas City, MO, 1994.

EuDaly, Kevin N., "White River", *CTC Board Railroads Illustrated*, Hyrail Productions, Denver, CO, December, 1991, pp. 16-33.

Feuge, Reuben M., "The Texas & Pacific-Missouri Pacific Terminal Railroad in New Orleans, Part 1," *The Eagle*, MPHS, Spring, 1990.

George, Raymond B., Jr., *Missouri-Kansas-Texas Lines in Color*, Morning Sun Books, Inc., Edison, NJ, 1994, p. 61.

Gray, George F., "The Texas Special," *Passenger Train Journal*, PTJ Publishing Co., Waukesha, WI, February, 1984, pp. 25-38.

Hartley, Scott, "An Exposition of E's," *Passenger Train Journal*, PTJ Publishing Co., Waukesha, WI, August, 1986.

Hoss, William L., "Passenger Train Operations at Kansas City, MO, September 18, 1965," *The Eagle*, MPHS, Fall, 1990, pp. 19-20.

Kohler, Steve and Ray, Tom, "The Mississippi River & Bonne Terre," *Model Railroader*, Kalmbach Publishing Co., Waukesha, WI, May, 1990, pp. 73-74.

Kuchinsky, Wayne, "Kansas City! Her Trains, Her Railroads, Her Stations," *Passenger Train Journal*, PTJ Publishing Co., Waukesha, WI, October, 1988.

Leeman, Wayne, "City's Last Commuter Train Succumbs to Changing Times," *St. Louis Post-Dispatch*, Pulitzer Publishing Co., St. Louis, MO, December 10, 1961.

Leeman, Wayne, "Wayne Leeman's St. Louis Union Station Scrapbook," *Trains Magazine*, Kalmbach Publishing Co., Milwaukee, WI, March, 1978.

MacGregor, Bruce and Benson, Ted, *Portrait of a Silver Lady*, Pruett Publishing Company, Boulder, CO, 1970, 1972, pp. 22-23.

Missouri Pacific Lines public timetables, 1933-1968 (various).

Moore, Jerry, "Missouri Pacific Trains 125 and 126," *The Eagle*, MPHS, Winter, 1990, pp. 14-21.

"MoPac's Delta Eagle", *The Eagle*, MPHS, Fall, 1982, pp. 4-13.

Morgan, David P., "The Most Talked About Train in the Country," *Trains Magazine*, Kalmbach Publishing Co., Milwaukee, WI, January, 1975, pp. 33-35.

Morgan, David P., "Who Shot the Passenger Train," *Trains Magazine*, Kalmbach Publishing Co., Milwaukee, WI, April, 1959.

Pennypacker, Bert, "Budd Before the Zephyr," *Trains Magazine*, Kalmbach Publishing Co., Milwaukee, WI, April, 1973, pp. 24-28.

Pitts, Jerry and Ramsey, Allan, "Wichita, The Sunflower and More," *The Eagle*, MPHS, Summer, 1987, pp. 7-11.

Randall, W. David and Anderson, William G., *The Official Pullman-Standard Library, Vol. 15*, RPC Publications, Godfrey, IL, 1994.

Ranks, Harold E. and Kratville, William W., *The Union Pacific Streamliners*, Kratville Publications, 1974.

Ryker, Richard, "MP Passenger Car Service/Service Changes," MPHS collection.

Sarno, Don and Shacklette, Norbert, "The Trains (and Trackage and Stations and Bridges) of St. Louis, Part 1," *Passenger Train Journal*, PTJ Publishing Co., Waukesha, WI, June, 1990.

"Those Esthetic E's," *Our GM Scrapbook*, Kalmbach Publishing Co., Milwaukee, WI, 1971, p. 31.

"Two New Streamlined Trains to be Ordered," *Missouri Pacific Lines Magazine*, February, 1941.

Walker, Dale L., "A Brief History of the St. Louis, Iron Mountain and Southern Railroad Company, 1851-1917, Part 2," *The Eagle*, MPHS, Summer, 1992.

Wayman, Norbury L., *St. Louis Union Station and Its Railroads*, The Evelyn E. Newman Group, St. Louis, MO, 1987.

World Almanac, 1941, 1949.

INDEX

126